Feminine Ancient Blessings

The Forbidden Feminine Codes To Heal, Manifest, and Awaken Your True Power

Codex Occulto

© **Copyright 2025 by Codex Occulto - All rights reserved.**

This publication provides accurate and reliable information on the subject matter discussed. It is sold with the understanding that the publisher is not offering legal, accounting, or professional services. For such advice, consult a qualified expert.

No part of this document may be copied, reproduced, stored, or shared - electronically or in print - without written permission from the publisher. All rights reserved.

The content is presented as-is, with no guarantees. The publisher assumes no responsibility for any loss, damage, or consequences resulting from the use or misuse of the information provided.

Trademarks mentioned are the property of their respective owners and are used for identification purposes only. This publication is not affiliated with them.

All copyrights remain with their respective authors unless held by the publisher.

Table of Contents

The Forgotten Feminine - Reclaiming Sacred Memory.. 7
Chapter 1: The Divine Feminine Archetype Through History..................... 13
    The Many Faces of the Goddess..13
    The Feminine Lost and Found..14
    Reawakening the Archetype Within..14
Chapter 2: The Womb as Portal... 16
    The Womb Beyond Biology.. 16
    The Womb as an Oracle.. 17
    The Womb as Cauldron of Creation... 18
    Closing Invitation... 19
Chapter 3: Cycles, Seasons, and Moon Codes.. 20
    The Moon as Mirror.. 20
    Seasonal Wisdom and the Feminine Body.. 21
    Tracking and Trusting Your Inner Cycle.. 22
    Closing Invitation... 23
Chapter 4: The Sacred Art of Slowness.. 25
    Rest as Resistance and Restoration... 25
    Receiving as a Spiritual Practice.. 26
    Trusting the Timing of Life.. 27
    Closing Invitation... 28
Chapter 5: Blood as Blessing: The Hidden Power of Menstruation........... 33
    Menstruation in Ancient Cultures...33
    The Cycle as an Energetic Map... 34
    Blood as Medicine and Ritual.. 35
    Closing Invitation... 36
Chapter 6: The Heart Field: Feminine Emotional Wisdom.......................... 38
    The Heart as Emotional Intelligence.. 38
    Softness as Strength.. 39
    Fierce Compassion and the Boundaries of the Heart....................................40
    Closing Invitation... 41

Chapter 7: Breast, Belly & Breath: Feminine Energy Centers 42
The Breasts: Nourishment, Giving, and Receiving 42
The Belly: Intuition, Creation, and Inner Power 43
The Breath: Presence, Life Force, and Emotional Alchemy 44
Closing Invitation 45

Chapter 8: The Voice as Vibration: Chanting, Storytelling, and Spoken Blessing 46
Chanting and the Power of Sound 46
The Feminine Art of Storytelling 47
Spoken Blessing and the Energetics of Intention 48
Closing Invitation 49

Chapter 9: The Blessing Bowl Ceremony: An Old Ritual for Releasing and Receiving 55
The Bowl as Sacred Vessel 55
Ritual for Release: Pouring Out the Old 56
Ritual for Receiving: Inviting the New 57
Closing Invitation 58

Chapter 10: Earth Offerings & Elemental Prayer: Working with Water, Fire, Air, and Earth 59
Earth: Anchoring, Belonging, and Physical Prayer 59
Water: Emotion, Intuition, and Fluid Prayer 60
Fire: Transformation, Passion, and Devotional Flame 61
Air: Breath, Thought, and Invisible Communion 62
Closing Invitation 63

Chapter 11: Feminine Circle Magic: Why Women Gathered - And How We Can Again 64
The Ancient Roots of Women's Circles 64
The Medicine of Being Witnessed 65
Creating and Holding Modern-Day Circles 66
Closing Invitation 67

Chapter 12: The Rite of Reclamation: A Guided Solo Ritual for Returning to Your Feminine Essence 69
Preparing the Sacred Space 69
The Three Gates: Descent, Stillness, and Emergence 70
Integrating the Ceremony into Daily Life 72

Chapter 13: From Suppression to Sovereignty: Healing the Wound of Being "Too Much" or "Not Enough" 77
    The Roots of Suppression 77
    The Journey of Healing and Remembering 78
    Sovereignty in Action: Living Unapologetically 79
    Closing Invitation 80

Chapter 14: Living in Ceremony: Everyday Acts as Sacred Gestures 82
    The Power of Intention in the Everyday 82
    Creating Personal Rituals That Matter 83
    Sacred Objects and Anchors of Devotion 84
    Closing Invitation 85

Chapter 15: The Feminine in Relationship: Boundaries, Magnetism, and Emotional Intimacy 87
    Boundaries as Sacred Containers 87
    The Power of Feminine Magnetism 88
    Emotional Intimacy and the Art of Vulnerable Expression 89
    Closing Invitation 90

Chapter 16: Creative Flow as Channel: Art, Dance, and Intuition as Forms of Divine Download 92
    Creativity as Feminine Intelligence 92
    Embodied Creation: Movement and Dance 93
    Intuition as the Creative Muse 94
    Closing Invitation 95

Chapter 17: Raising Feminine Children (Regardless of Gender): Nurturing Presence, Softness, and Inner Knowing 101
    Honoring Emotions as Sacred Language 101
    Fostering Intuition, Imagination, and Inner Trust 102
    Teaching Boundaries, Consent, and Embodied Self-Respect 103
    Closing Invitation 105

Chapter 18: The Feminine Leader: Leading Without Force: Influence Through Energy, Space, and Vision 106
    Energetic Leadership: Presence Before Performance 106
    Holding Space Instead of Taking Control 107
    Leading with Vision and Embodiment 108
    Closing Invitation 109

Chapter 19: Creating Blessing Altars: Personal Sacred Spaces That Shift Your Frequency... **111**
    The Meaning and Energy of an Altar... 111
    How to Create a Feminine Blessing Altar..112
    Using Your Altar to Shift Frequency and Manifest Intention..........114
    Closing Invitation... 115

Chapter 20: Your Feminine Legacy: A Final Guided Practice to Anchor Your Own Ancient Blessing into the World..**116**
    Listening to the Thread of Your Lineage... 116
    Living as the Blessing You Are..117
    Anchoring Your Blessing: A Guided Practice....................................118
    Closing Words... 120

The Forgotten Feminine - Reclaiming Sacred Memory

There is a memory in your bones older than your name.

It is the memory of women draped in moonlight, whispering prayers to rivers. Of grandmothers pressing herbs into hands. Of priestesses dancing barefoot in temples before time turned sacredness into superstition. This memory is not lost - it is simply waiting to be remembered.

We live in a world where the feminine has long been distorted, suppressed, or misunderstood. In the great machinery of modern life, the subtle, the soft, the cyclical, and the sacred have been labeled as weaknesses. We were told to move faster, think harder, and achieve more. And in doing so, we began to forget. We forgot how to feel, how to listen, how to flow.

"Feminine Ancient Blessings" is an invitation to remember - not just intellectually, but viscerally. To return to the sacred wisdom that pulses beneath the surface of our lives. This is not merely a book of knowledge, but a map of reawakening.

The feminine is not a gender - it is an energy, an archetype, a presence that lives in all of us. It is the womb of creation, the heart of compassion, the rhythm of the earth. Whether you are woman, man, or beyond the binary, the feminine calls to be acknowledged, honored, and embodied.

In these pages, we will walk together through ancient lineages of feminine wisdom - from myth to moon, from blood to breath, from ritual to everyday sacredness. We will listen to the voices of the ancestors, dance with the elements, and remember what it means to live in harmony with ourselves, each other, and the cosmos.

This is not about returning to the past. This is about reviving what the past still wants to offer us: the blessings that have been buried, hidden, or silenced. These blessings are still here. And they are still alive.

You do not need to seek permission to reclaim them.

You are the altar. You are the priestess. You are the blessing.

Let us begin.

PART I: THE WISDOM OF THE MOTHERS

Chapter 1: The Divine Feminine Archetype Through History

Across time and culture, the Divine Feminine has worn many faces. She has been revered as goddess, mother, oracle, queen, lover, wild woman, and healer. Though her names changed with language and geography, the essence of her archetype remained: a force of creation, destruction, nurturance, and transformation.

To awaken her now, we must first look back. We must remember who she was before she was hidden.

The Many Faces of the Goddess

In ancient Egypt, she was **Isis**, the mother of magic and mystery. Her wings wrapped around the world, and her tears of mourning restored the body of her beloved Osiris. Isis was not just a wife or mother - she was a protector of the dead and guide to the afterlife, a symbol of divine femininity in its fullness: fierce, faithful, and wise.

In Sumeria, long before the gods of patriarchal pantheons rose to dominance, there was **Inanna** - Queen of Heaven and Earth. Inanna descended into the underworld not as a victim, but as a sovereign. Her myth tells of self-stripping, death, and rebirth. She is the feminine that dares to face shadow, to surrender identity, and to rise again more whole.

In Yoruba traditions, she is **Yemanjá**, the ocean mother. She brings life and takes it. She flows with the tide, cradles the unborn, and listens to the songs of sorrow and joy sung by women on the shores. Yemanjá reminds us that the feminine is water: deep, emotional, shifting, vast.

And then, there is **Mary**, often sanitized into docility, yet hiding immense spiritual power. Mary is the Madonna - the one who births the divine into human form. She is the rose blooming in the desert of patriarchal narratives, holding a line of sacred femininity through centuries of suppression. The Black Madonnas of Europe, her darker-skinned depictions, hint at even older, earthier roots.

These goddesses and sacred figures are not relics of mythology; they are archetypes that live in our psyche and cells. Their stories carry encoded wisdom that transcends religion or era. They offer us mirrors through which to see ourselves.

The Feminine Lost and Found

With the rise of monotheistic religions and patriarchal structures, the Divine Feminine was systematically diminished. She was cast out of the temple, silenced in scriptures, and vilified as temptation. God became "He," and the feminine became either virgin or whore - no longer whole, no longer sovereign.

Temples to the goddess were razed. Priestesses were exiled. Wombs became property. Intuition became hysteria. And yet, underground and in secret, her worship continued. In folk traditions, in herbal medicine, in lullabies, in midwifery, in dreams.

The repression of the feminine wasn't just spiritual - it was psychological and cultural. It taught us to distrust our inner voice, to prioritize logic over feeling, productivity over presence, dominance over relationship. We began to sever ourselves from the Earth, from our own rhythms, from the mystery.

But the feminine does not die. She waits. She dreams. She returns.

Reawakening the Archetype Within

The Divine Feminine is not merely "out there" in statues and stories. She is within you. When you nurture, when you create, when you cry without shame or dance without reason - she moves through you. When you listen to your body's no or honor your need to rest, you are invoking her.

The ancient archetypes are not meant to be worshiped passively, but embodied actively. Inanna's descent becomes your willingness to face your shadows. Isis' magic becomes your capacity to mend what has been broken. Yemanjá's waters become your ability to feel and forgive. Mary's presence becomes your offering of grace.

To work with these energies is to become more whole. Not just more "feminine" in appearance, but more alive in truth.

You do not need to become someone else to awaken the Divine Feminine. You only need to peel back the layers of forgetting. To soften. To feel. To remember.

She is not a fantasy. She is a frequency. And she is calling you now.

Chapter 2: The Womb as Portal

There is a sacred intelligence within the human body that has long been forgotten, hidden beneath centuries of control, shame, and disconnection. At the center of this intelligence lies the womb - a physical organ, yes, but also a spiritual portal. Whether we have a physical womb or not, whether it functions or not, its energetic counterpart exists in all of us. The womb space is not just about reproduction; it is the seat of creation, intuition, and life force. It is the original altar, the holy vessel, the site of memory and mystery. To reclaim the power of the womb is to reawaken our ability to create not only life but also art, dreams, boundaries, and truth.

The Womb Beyond Biology

Many people associate the womb solely with the biological function of reproduction. While this is one of its physical roles, it is only a fragment of the full picture. The womb is a multidimensional space. It is both physical and energetic. It holds the power to gestate not only babies, but also visions, relationships, and transformations.

Even those who no longer have a physical womb - or never had one - can still connect with the womb space energetically. In many spiritual traditions, this space is referred to as the hara, sacral center, or yoni temple. It is the second chakra in yogic systems, governing creativity, sexuality, and flow. In Taoist and Tantric teachings, it is a reservoir of "jing" - vital essence that fuels longevity, clarity, and inner knowing.

To tap into this space, we don't need to perform elaborate rituals. What we need is presence. Attention. Listening. When we bring awareness to our lower belly, we often discover emotions, sensations, and memories that the mind has overlooked. This is because the womb, like the heart, stores experiences - especially those related to connection, betrayal, intimacy, and trust. Modern society has taught us to live in our heads. But feminine wisdom lives in the body - particularly in the womb. When we bypass this space, we lose access to our deepest knowing. When we return to it, we begin to remember not only who we are, but also what we are here to create.

The Womb as an Oracle

The womb is a portal to intuition. Not the kind of intuition that flashes like a lightning bolt in the mind, but the slow, steady hum of inner truth. It speaks in sensations: a tightening when something feels off, a spaciousness when something is aligned. It does not shout - it whispers. And the world is often too loud for us to hear.

Many women and womb-bearers have been conditioned to distrust this inner voice. We were told to rationalize our feelings, to suppress our gut instincts, to seek approval outside of ourselves. Over time, we became disconnected from our internal compass. We started asking others for answers that could only be found within. To reconnect with womb wisdom, we must create space for silence. We must cultivate slowness, breath, and attention. Meditation, belly breathing, pelvic floor awareness, and simply resting a hand on the lower abdomen are all simple ways to begin. As we return to this center, we may find grief there - grief for all the times we overrode our truth, abandoned our boundaries, or allowed our sacredness to be devalued. But we may also find strength. The womb holds resilience. It remembers our ancestors, their dreams and heartbreaks. It is a well of power that cannot be taken - only forgotten. And it is always ready to be remembered.

One powerful practice is womb journaling. Sit in quietude with your hands on your belly, breathe deeply into this space, and ask: What do you need me to know? Then write without censoring. You may be surprised by what emerges. Often, the womb speaks in symbols, poetry, or simple truths:

Rest. Say no. Paint. Sing. Walk away. Over time, this dialogue becomes a sacred friendship.

The Womb as Cauldron of Creation

Creation is not limited to childbirth. Every idea you birth, every boundary you hold, every truth you speak from your center is an act of creation. The womb space is the cauldron where raw energy becomes form. In mythology, this is the space of the Great Mother - the one who gestates galaxies in her belly, who spins stars from silence, who shapes matter from mystery.

When we align with our womb space, we tap into a wellspring of creative energy that is not forceful or linear. It is cyclical, intuitive, and deeply rooted. It is not about "doing more" - it is about allowing more. We do not push the rose to bloom. We create the conditions for blooming to unfold. This kind of creation honors rest as much as action. It honors void as much as vision. Just like the menstrual cycle contains phases of shedding, stillness, building, and release, our creative cycles mirror these rhythms. Many people suffer creative blocks not because they lack talent, but because they resist the natural ebb and flow. They try to produce in the void phase or force inspiration during rest.

Honoring the womb means honoring your cycles. It means trusting the timing of your inner seasons. Some days you will bleed - emotionally or energetically. Other days you will spark with clarity. Both are sacred. Both are part of the process. You can activate your creative womb energy through movement: belly dance, hip circles, grounding walks, even freeform dance in private. You can also feed this space with beauty - aromatherapy, moon rituals, or bathing with intention. The womb is deeply responsive to pleasure, not in the narrow sense of sexual pleasure, but in the broad sense of aliveness. When we allow beauty, softness, and joy to touch us, the womb opens.

In a world that glorifies mental intelligence and productivity, womb-centered creation is revolutionary. It is less about control and more about co-creation with life. It says: I trust my timing. I trust my knowing. I trust the womb of the world to guide me.

Closing Invitation

The womb is not a concept. It is not an idea to think about. It is a place to enter, to feel, to honor. Whether you enter it through meditation, movement, journaling, or ritual, the invitation is always open. This is the seat of the feminine blessings - the place where life begins, where truth resides, where the mystery lives.

To remember the womb is to remember your power.

And when you remember your power, you begin to remember the ancient feminine within you.

Let her speak. Let her lead. Let her create.

Chapter 3: Cycles, Seasons, and Moon Codes

Long before clocks, calendars, or productivity apps, women attuned themselves to the rhythms of nature. The moon, the tides, the changing seasons - these were the original timekeepers. Life was not measured in hours but in cycles. Blood, bloom, rest, and rebirth were not separate from the sacred; they were the sacred. In a world that now demands constant action, we've forgotten that power is not always about pushing - it is often about aligning. This chapter invites you to reawaken the ancient feminine wisdom of cyclical living. To remember that your body, your energy, and your creativity are not machines - they are moons.

The Moon as Mirror

The moon has always been a companion to the feminine. She waxes and wanes, disappears and returns. She holds the mystery of time, emotion, and inner change. In nearly every ancient culture, the moon was seen as feminine - associated with goddesses, fertility, intuition, and magic. Ancient women tracked her phases not just for agriculture or navigation, but for self-understanding. They knew that her cycle was their cycle.

The average menstrual cycle, like the lunar cycle, spans about 28 to 29 days. This is not coincidence - it is cosmic design. Each phase of the moon mirrors an energetic phase within the menstrual or creative cycle. When we align ourselves with the moon, we're not engaging in a trend. We're returning to a forgotten language - the language of resonance.

The new moon, cloaked in darkness, represents the void. It is the phase of introspection, release, and rest. Like the menstrual phase, it is a time to turn inward, to let go of what no longer serves, to make space for the new.

The waxing moon is the phase of building energy, hope, and intention. It mirrors the follicular phase of the cycle, when energy rises and clarity begins to take shape. It is a time for dreaming, planting, beginning.

The full moon is illumination - peak energy, ovulation, abundance. It is a time to shine, to express, to be seen. Emotions are heightened, insights crystallize, and the veil between worlds feels thin. In many traditions, women gathered in circles under the full moon to share stories, rituals, and prayers.

The waning moon is a time of refinement, discernment, and preparation for release. Like the luteal phase, it often brings up what is unresolved. It invites us to look inward again, to tidy our inner and outer world before the descent.

Even those who do not menstruate can still align with the moon. The body responds to lunar energy regardless of biology. You might notice changes in your sleep, mood, or creative impulses depending on the moon phase. By simply tracking how you feel during each phase, you begin to rebuild this intuitive connection.

Living by the moon is not superstition - it is pattern recognition. It is remembrance.

Seasonal Wisdom and the Feminine Body

Just as the moon carries monthly rhythms, the Earth moves through her own grand cycle each year. Spring, summer, autumn, and winter are not just changes in weather; they are stages of a feminine journey. Each season corresponds to an inner archetype and an energetic invitation.

Spring is the maiden. She is fresh, curious, and bold. This is the energy of beginning anew - of setting intentions, taking first steps, playing with possibility. In the body, this is like the post-menstrual phase when energy begins to rise and the world feels full of color again. Creativity sparks. Vision becomes clear. There's a sense of awakening.

Summer is the mother. She is full, nurturing, and expressive. This is the energy of giving, blooming, and sustaining. In the body, this is the ovulatory phase - a time of openness, connection, and outward movement. It's a potent moment for collaboration, leadership, and generosity. But it also requires boundaries, for even the sun must eventually set.

Autumn is the enchantress, or the wild woman. She sees through illusions. She prepares for the descent. This is the luteal phase - a time of shedding, shadow work, and discernment. Emotions rise. Truths come to the surface. This phase is often the most misunderstood, as it demands honesty and space. But it is rich with insight and power.

Winter is the crone. The wise woman. The still point. This is the menstrual phase, or for non-menstruating bodies, the energetic void. It is a time of rest, of listening deeply, of dreaming in the dark. It is the womb of the year - a time to retreat, reflect, and restore.

When we live in accordance with these seasonal energies, we stop fighting ourselves. We stop expecting constant productivity and begin to honor the natural ebb and flow. We recognize that there are times to bloom and times to be buried. Times to speak and times to be silent. Times to give and times to gather.

To practice seasonal living, you don't need to change your entire lifestyle. Start by noticing: How do you feel in each season? What foods, colors, or practices nourish you? Which times of year feel expansive, and which feel inward? Allow your body to be your guide.

Tracking and Trusting Your Inner Cycle

The path to living cyclically begins with awareness. Whether you menstruate or not, whether you track the moon or the seasons, the key is to attune to your own inner rhythm. This means moving from external scheduling to internal sensing.

Begin by keeping a cycle journal. Each day, note how you feel physically, emotionally, mentally, and spiritually. What's your energy like? What do you crave? How's your sleep? Over time, patterns will emerge. You'll begin to see your own moon. Your own seasons. Your own language of energy.

You may discover that certain phases are more creative, while others are more contemplative. You may find that your emotional landscape shifts in a predictable rhythm. This awareness empowers you to plan your life in harmony with your nature - not in opposition to it.

This also allows for compassionate self-care. Instead of judging yourself for being tired, unmotivated, or emotional, you begin to recognize these states as part of your sacred rhythm. You learn when to push and when to pause. When to speak and when to listen. You honor the intelligence of your inner tides.

If you do menstruate, tracking your menstrual cycle becomes a powerful spiritual and practical tool. Each phase - menstrual, follicular, ovulatory, and luteal - holds unique gifts. The bleed is not an inconvenience; it is a clearing. Ovulation is not just about fertility; it is about presence. PMS is not a curse; it is a call to recalibrate.

By syncing your tasks, rituals, and self-care to your inner rhythm, you begin to live in harmony with your own nature. You become a student of your own sacred timing.

Closing Invitation

Cycles are not obstacles to overcome - they are invitations to align. In a world that moves in straight lines and deadlines, reclaiming your cyclical nature is an act of feminine remembrance.

You are not meant to bloom all the time.

You are meant to wax and wane, to rise and rest, to spiral into deeper layers of yourself.

Just like the moon. Just like the Earth.

When you honor your cycles, you come home to yourself.

Let this be your new rhythm: slow, sacred, and sovereign.

Chapter 4: The Sacred Art of Slowness

We live in a world that worships speed. Productivity has become a measure of worth, and busyness a badge of honor. In this fast-moving current, slowness is often mistaken for laziness, and rest is treated as a luxury instead of a necessity. But ancient feminine wisdom tells a different story. It reminds us that the sacred moves slowly. That deep roots grow in stillness. That true creation takes time, darkness, and surrender. In a culture obsessed with doing, the feminine invites us to simply be. She whispers not in urgency, but in patience. Not in hustle, but in presence. This chapter is an invitation to reclaim slowness as a sacred act, a return to rhythm, and a powerful feminine blessing.

Rest as Resistance and Restoration

In ancient times, rest was woven into the fabric of daily life. The cycles of the moon, the ebb of the tides, the turning of seasons all pointed to a rhythm that allowed for retreat as much as action. Sacred sites were not only places of prayer, but places of pause. The feminine did not rush - she ripened.

Today, we are told to move faster, do more, and ignore the body's need for rest. We drink caffeine instead of slowing down. We power through exhaustion. We feel guilt for sleeping in, for canceling plans, for taking time for ourselves. And yet, beneath this constant motion is a collective fatigue. An aching. A hunger for softness.

Rest is not optional. It is vital. And it is deeply sacred. When we rest, we allow the nervous system to reset. We open the door to intuition. We step out of survival mode and back into presence. The mind slows. The heart opens. The body begins to trust us again.

For women and feminine beings, rest is especially important. The womb and the heart - our primary centers of feminine energy - require spaciousness to speak. When we are always moving, always pushing, we cannot hear their wisdom. Rest becomes the portal through which we remember.

This is not about abandoning action or goals. It is about anchoring them in something deeper. True feminine power is not hurried - it is rooted. When we rest, we reconnect to that root. We remember that our value is not tied to our output. We are already worthy, already enough.

Simple practices like taking a nap, sitting in silence, turning off notifications, or doing nothing for ten minutes a day are radical in today's culture. But they are also revolutionary. They are how we return to ourselves. How we say to the world: I will not be rushed through my own life.

Receiving as a Spiritual Practice

Slowness is not just about rest. It is also about receiving. In the masculine-coded world we live in, giving is praised, while receiving is often overlooked or even shamed. We are taught to strive, to pursue, to make things happen. But the feminine path is one of magnetism. She does not chase - she attracts.

Receiving is not passive. It is deeply active. It requires presence, openness, and trust. It asks us to soften the grip of control and allow life to move toward us. This can be terrifying for those of us taught to equate safety with control. And yet, some of the most beautiful things come when we step out of the way.

To receive is to open your body, your heart, your spirit. It is to say: I trust the timing. I trust the process. I trust that I am worthy of goodness without earning it through exhaustion.

The womb is a receiver. It does not go out and grab - it draws in. It opens. It holds. It waits. The heart, too, receives. Not through force, but through receptivity. When we allow ourselves to receive - support, affection, abundance, rest - we step into the feminine current of life.

Many of us struggle with receiving because we were taught that we must always give. Especially women. We were taught to be caretakers, to pour ourselves out without ever filling back up. But this leads to depletion. Bitterness. Burnout.

Receiving is how we restore the balance. It is how we fill the sacred cup. You can begin this practice by noticing how you respond to compliments. Do you deflect or diminish them? Try simply saying, "Thank you." Allow kindness in. Let someone help you. Let the sun warm your face. Let the Earth support your weight as you lie down.

There is an elegance in allowing. A grace in opening. When we live in slowness, we remember how to receive - not just from others, but from the universe itself. We become vessels for the blessings that were always waiting for us.

Trusting the Timing of Life

Perhaps the most challenging aspect of slowness is trusting in timing. In a culture of instant gratification, we want results now. We want healing to be fast. Success to be overnight. Love to be immediate. But the feminine understands something deeper: true growth takes time.

Seeds germinate in the dark. Babies grow in the womb. Dreams ripen slowly. Nature does not rush, yet everything unfolds perfectly. When we slow down, we begin to sync with this divine rhythm. We stop forcing outcomes. We start listening for right timing.

The ancient feminine teaches us to honor the gestation phase - the time between intention and manifestation. This is the time when it looks like nothing is happening, but everything is being rearranged beneath the surface. This is the space of trust.

Trust is not blind belief. It is a deep knowing that what is meant for you cannot miss you. It is the ability to rest without urgency. To wait without anxiety. To allow space for mystery.

When we do not trust timing, we fall into comparison and fear. We believe we are behind, broken, or failing. But when we return to the feminine pace, we realize we are exactly where we are meant to be. Life is not linear - it is cyclical. What looks like delay is often preparation. What feels like stagnation is often deep integration.

Slowness is the path of trust. It is how we stay rooted in a world of rush. It is how we listen for divine timing, rather than imposing our own.

You might try a simple ritual: write down something you desire - a project, a relationship, a healing - and place it under a stone, a bowl, or inside a box. Close your eyes and say, "I surrender this to divine timing. I release the need to rush. I trust the unfolding." Then go about your life. Do what needs doing. But hold that seed in your heart - not with urgency, but with quiet knowing.

Closing Invitation

The sacred art of slowness is not about doing nothing. It is about doing everything from a place of depth, presence, and trust. It is how we come back into rhythm with the Earth, the moon, and ourselves.

Let your life be less about the race and more about the ritual.

Let your rest be holy.

Let your receiving be graceful.

Let your trust be fierce.

Slowness is not the absence of power - it is its embodiment. And in remembering how to slow down, we remember how to live in a way that is fully alive.

PART II: BLESSINGS THROUGH THE BODY

Chapter 5: Blood as Blessing: The Hidden Power of Menstruation

There is perhaps no aspect of the feminine body more misunderstood, silenced, or shamed than menstrual blood. In ancient times, this blood was seen as sacred - an expression of life force, a sign of a woman's connection to the cosmos, the Earth, and the cycles of creation. But somewhere along the way, the narrative shifted. Menstruation became taboo. It was hidden, medicalized, and stigmatized. Its power was forgotten. This chapter seeks to reclaim the sacredness of menstrual blood - not only as a biological process but as an energetic and spiritual gateway. Whether you menstruate now, have in the past, or simply carry this ancestral coding within your body or lineage, the invitation is the same: to remember that your blood is not a burden. It is a blessing.

Menstruation in Ancient Cultures

Long before the age of synthetic pads and sterile language, menstruation was treated with reverence. Many Indigenous cultures recognized the menstrual cycle as a mirror of the moon's cycle and the Earth's fertility. Bleeding women were often considered spiritually potent, not dirty or impure. Their withdrawal from daily tasks during their moon time wasn't a punishment - it was a practice of power, rest, and vision.

In ancient Mesopotamia, priestesses were often menstruating women who would enter temples during their bleed to receive oracles and commune with the divine. In parts of Africa and the Americas, menstrual huts were used - not as isolation, but as intentional sanctuaries where women could rest, dream, and support one another. In some Native American traditions, women on their moon time were considered so spiritually powerful that their prayers were believed to be amplified.

This connection between menstruation and spiritual power was widespread. It wasn't always spoken in words we would recognize now, but it lived in practice. In rhythm. In ritual. The blood was seen not as waste, but as wisdom. A sign that the body was aligned with the natural order.

With the rise of patriarchal religious systems and colonial expansion, this reverence was turned into fear. Menstrual blood became "unclean," and the power of the bleeding woman was viewed as dangerous. What had been a source of awe became a source of shame. That wound still echoes in the way our cultures treat menstruation today - through euphemisms, embarrassment, and invisibility.

To reclaim menstruation as sacred is to confront that shame and rewrite the story. It is to say: this blood is not weakness. It is a sign of connection, creation, and transformation.

The Cycle as an Energetic Map

Beyond the physical shedding, menstruation represents an intricate dance of hormones, energy, and archetypes. The menstrual cycle isn't a flat line - it is a spiraling rhythm that repeats each month, offering different gifts in each phase. To understand the cycle as an energetic map is to reconnect with the inner seasons of the feminine body.

Menstruation (Day 1–5): This is the winter phase, a time of release, death, and deep intuition. The veil is thin during this time, and many women report increased dreams, spiritual insight, and emotional truth rising to the surface. The body asks for slowness. It sheds not only physical lining but emotional and energetic residue as well. It is a time to retreat, reflect, and restore.

Follicular Phase (Day 6–13): This is spring - renewal, hope, energy returning. Estrogen begins to rise, and with it comes creativity, optimism, and a desire to start fresh. This is a wonderful time to plant seeds - both literal and metaphorical. New projects, intentions, and ideas flourish here. It's a phase of movement and curiosity.

Ovulation (Day 14–17): This is summer - peak vitality, magnetism, and outward expression. The body is open to connection, and so is the spirit. Many women feel most confident, social, and productive during this phase. It is a time of fertility, not just in terms of reproduction, but also in manifestation and joy. Communication flows. Visibility feels natural.

Luteal Phase (Day 18–28): This is autumn - the descent. Energy begins to turn inward again. Progesterone rises and then drops. Sensitivity increases. Intuition sharpens. If we ignore the need for reflection during this phase, we may experience irritation, exhaustion, or emotional overwhelm. But if we honor it, it becomes a time of powerful insight and truth-telling.

Each phase is a teacher. Each one brings a different blessing. When we begin to live in alignment with this cycle - tracking our energy, shifting our self-care, and respecting our body's needs - we access a level of intelligence that is ancient and personal. We begin to trust ourselves in a new way.

This cyclical awareness is especially powerful for those who experience menstrual challenges like pain, irregularity, or emotional turbulence. These symptoms are often messages - signals that the body wants to be heard, nourished, and supported in a different way. Reclaiming menstruation as sacred means approaching it not as a problem to be fixed, but as a rhythm to be honored.

Blood as Medicine and Ritual

The menstrual blood itself holds energy. In ancient traditions, it was not only symbolic but used in ritual and healing. Blood was returned to the Earth as a form of offering, a way of completing the cycle of giving and receiving. It was believed to fertilize soil, feed the land, and strengthen the relationship between body and Earth.

Today, many women are returning to the practice of blood rituals - not in a theatrical or dogmatic way, but as an intimate act of reclamation. Collecting menstrual blood (using a menstrual cup or cloth) and offering it to plants or the Earth can be a powerful way to reconnect to this ancient wisdom. It is a quiet ceremony of gratitude. A moment of remembering.

You don't have to offer your blood to the Earth to honor its sacredness. Simply acknowledging its presence with reverence, lighting a candle during your bleed, creating art from your emotions, or journaling your inner experiences during each cycle can become a ritual. What matters is the energy of intention. You are no longer ignoring it - you are communing with it.

Menstrual blood is also energetically cleansing. It can help release stored emotions, unresolved grief, or creative stagnation. When we bleed consciously, we allow the body to reset. The act of menstruation becomes not just a shedding, but a sacred surrender.

It's also worth noting that for those who no longer menstruate - whether through menopause, medical reasons, or choice - the energy of the cycle still lives in the body. The inner rhythm remains. The archetypes of the inner seasons can still be honored through intention, visualization, and ritual. Moon phases, especially the new and full moon, can serve as energetic guides for tuning into this rhythm.

Closing Invitation

The power of the feminine does not lie in conformity. It lies in remembering what has been silenced. In claiming what was once feared. In transforming shame into sovereignty.

Your blood is not shameful. It is sacred.

Your cycle is not a flaw. It is a portal.

When you listen to your bleeding body, you remember something the world forgot: that life is not linear, that power is not constant output, and that mystery lives in your very bones.

Let your cycle be your ceremony.

Let your blood be your blessing.

Let your body be your oracle.

Chapter 6: The Heart Field: Feminine Emotional Wisdom

At the center of the feminine body and soul is the heart - a vast, radiant field of feeling, connection, and intuition. The heart is not only an organ of love but a gateway to emotional truth. In a society that often teaches us to numb, rationalize, or harden ourselves, the feminine heart remembers a different way. It teaches us that emotions are not flaws to fix or distractions to overcome, but intelligent messengers. They are rivers that carry us toward authenticity, compassion, and wholeness. The heart is the seat of feminine wisdom because it feels before it knows, it softens before it speaks, and it opens even when it's afraid. To reclaim feminine power, we must reclaim the heart - not only as a metaphor, but as a living energy field through which we relate to ourselves, others, and the world.

The Heart as Emotional Intelligence

Emotions are not chaos - they are communication. Each emotion has its own frequency, purpose, and invitation. Anger can signal a boundary crossed. Sadness can open the door to release. Joy expands us. Fear protects us. Shame asks for deeper self-compassion. Yet many of us were not taught to listen to our emotions. We were taught to suppress, dismiss, or overanalyze them.

The feminine path does not bypass emotion. It honors it. Emotional intelligence is not about avoiding difficult feelings - it's about learning how to stay present with them, to understand their messages, and to move through them with grace. This is what the heart field teaches us: presence without judgment.

The heart holds memory - not just of events, but of emotional truths. It remembers the pain we couldn't express, the love we didn't receive, the joy we were afraid to feel. It also remembers the beauty we've forgotten. Reconnecting to the heart field is not about becoming fragile - it's about becoming attuned. When we are emotionally attuned, we stop reacting and start responding. We develop emotional sovereignty.

In ancient traditions, especially those rooted in goddess cultures and earth-based spirituality, emotions were seen as sacred forces, often personified as goddesses themselves. Aphrodite wasn't just the goddess of sensuality - she was the embodiment of emotional magnetism. Kuan Yin, the goddess of compassion, showed that divine power could be tender. Yemanjá, the ocean mother, held space for the emotional tides of grief and love alike.

We must return to this understanding: emotion is not a weakness. Emotion is feminine intelligence in motion.

Softness as Strength

One of the most radical acts in today's world is softness. In a society that values toughness, defensiveness, and self-containment, choosing softness requires tremendous courage. But softness is not passivity. It is not submission. It is a conscious choice to remain open when closing would be easier. It is a powerful force of the feminine heart.

The feminine does not armor up to protect herself - she learns to discern who is safe, where she can be soft, and when to draw a boundary that guards her softness like sacred ground. True feminine strength is not about domination or control - it is about presence. It is about being deeply rooted in the heart while remaining spacious enough to receive the world as it is.

Softness allows us to connect. When we are soft, we can feel more - yes - but we also hear more, intuit more, and understand more. Softness lets us meet others with empathy. It lets us meet ourselves with grace. It transforms conflict into dialogue and fear into curiosity.

In your own life, softness can be cultivated through daily presence: gentle self-touch, kind inner dialogue, slow breathing, or simply pausing before reacting. Ask yourself: How can I meet this moment with softness? What would softness look like right now?

There is a myth that feminine power is only fierce. But softness is a different kind of fierceness. It is the fierceness of choosing love even when it's hard. Of staying open even when the world tells you to shut down. Of trusting that tenderness is not something to overcome - it is something to embody.

Fierce Compassion and the Boundaries of the Heart

True compassion is not self-sacrifice. It is not allowing yourself to be depleted for the sake of others. The feminine heart knows that compassion must include the self. That healthy love requires healthy boundaries. This is the difference between martyrdom and sovereignty.

Fierce compassion is the ability to hold space without absorbing someone else's pain. It's the strength to say "no" with love. It's the wisdom to know when to walk away and when to stay present. The feminine heart is not naïve - it is discerning. It knows that to truly serve others, we must first be grounded in our own truth.

Many women have been taught that love means pleasing, fixing, or abandoning themselves. But the sacred feminine redefines love. She says: You can be kind and clear. You can be open and protected. You can care deeply and still choose yourself.

The heart field teaches us that compassion is not enabling. It is seeing someone clearly, meeting them with empathy, and still holding your own center. This requires inner work: healing codependency, dissolving the need to be liked, and tending to your own inner child who learned to equate love with overgiving.

Energetically, the heart has a powerful electromagnetic field - wider and stronger than that of the brain. It sends signals out into the world, and it receives information constantly. When we're attuned to our heart, we become more sensitive not only to emotions, but to truth. We can feel when something is off, even if the words sound right. We can sense when someone is authentic or hiding. This is the intuitive power of the heart field.

Practices like heart coherence breathing (inhaling into the heart space, exhaling gratitude or compassion) help to reset the nervous system and bring us back into this field. Holding a hand over the chest and simply saying "I'm here" can reestablish presence in moments of overwhelm. These small rituals remind us that the heart is not just a metaphor - it is a living compass.

Closing Invitation

To reclaim the feminine heart is to reclaim the wisdom of feeling. It is to walk the world with open eyes and an open chest. It is to stop numbing, and start noticing. To feel deeply, speak honestly, love fiercely, and rest in the knowledge that your emotions are not your enemies - they are your allies.

Let your heart be the altar. Let your feelings be the prayers.

Let your softness be your strength, and your boundaries be your sanctuary.

The feminine heart is not fragile. It is vast. It is ancient. And it remembers the way back to wholeness.

Chapter 7: Breast, Belly & Breath: Feminine Energy Centers

Within the feminine body lies a landscape of wisdom - an energetic map that holds memory, power, and presence. While much attention in spiritual teachings is given to the mind or the upper chakras, the ancient feminine tradition reminds us that the body is not just a vessel but a temple. Specifically, the breasts, belly, and breath form a sacred triad of energy centers that offer profound insight and healing. Each of these areas is not just biological, but vibrational. They are portals to feeling, intuition, nourishment, and grounded sensuality. When we reconnect with these centers - not from objectification but from reverence - we remember a truth that predates every wound: the body is divine, and every part of it speaks the language of the soul.

The Breasts: Nourishment, Giving, and Receiving

The breasts are among the most symbolically charged parts of the feminine body. In modern culture, they are often sexualized, scrutinized, or hidden. But long before they were commodified, the breasts were revered as sacred sources of nourishment, connection, and heart-centered wisdom.

In many ancient traditions, goddesses were depicted with full, open chests - not to seduce, but to symbolize abundance, generosity, and life-giving force. The breasts are located at the heart chakra, connecting them to love, compassion, and giving. But they are also receivers. Energetically, they absorb. They feel. They sense.

Many women carry stored tension, grief, or self-judgment in their chest. Tightness in the upper body is not just physical - it is emotional. When we have given too much without receiving, when we have silenced our own needs, when we have internalized shame around our bodies, the breasts remember. They hold.

Breast massage, heart opening breathwork, and conscious touch are powerful tools to reconnect with this part of ourselves. These practices are not about performance or appearance - they are acts of devotion. When we touch our breasts with love and presence, we reawaken the ability to receive. We remind ourselves that we are not here only to give endlessly - we are also here to be filled.

Breast awareness also reclaims sensuality as sacred. Sensuality is not just sexual - it is about being fully alive in the body. It is the ability to feel the sun on your skin, the texture of silk, the warmth of another's presence. When we reclaim our breasts as part of our whole-body consciousness, we begin to heal centuries of objectification and return to inner wholeness.

The Belly: Intuition, Creation, and Inner Power

The belly is the deep ocean of the feminine body. It is home to the womb, the gut, the center of gravity. It is where we digest food, emotions, and experiences. It is the seat of instinct and creative potential. And it is one of the most neglected and misunderstood parts of the body.

Culturally, the belly has been targeted with impossible ideals. Flat, tight, controlled - these are the messages we receive. But the feminine belly is meant to be round, soft, strong, and alive. It is the literal and symbolic center of creation. It expands with breath, with life, with emotion.

Within the belly lies the sacral chakra - the energy center associated with creativity, sexuality, and flow. When this area is blocked or shamed, we often experience disconnection from desire, difficulty expressing ourselves, or fear of our own power. Reclaiming the belly means reclaiming our creative force.

Start by simply placing your hands on your belly. Breathe into it. Feel it rise and fall. Notice any sensations or resistance. You might speak to it: What are you holding? What do you need? Over time, the belly will begin to speak back - through images, emotions, or sudden clarity.

Dance is another profound way to awaken the belly. Especially forms like belly dance, which were originally devotional movements, not performances. Hip circles, figure eights, and pelvic undulations activate this center and help move stuck energy. They invite us to feel powerful, sensual, and rooted.

The belly also holds ancestral memory. The eggs that would become each of us were formed inside our mother's womb while she was inside our grandmother's. This lineage lives in our bellies. When we heal our relationship with this center, we do not do so alone - we heal the line of women who came before us.

The belly is not a problem to be fixed. It is a portal to be honored. It is your center of gravity. Your seat of wisdom. Your ocean of becoming.

The Breath: Presence, Life Force, and Emotional Alchemy

Breath is the bridge between the seen and unseen. It is the first thing we do when we enter this world and the last thing we do when we leave it. It is both automatic and intentional, unconscious and conscious. And yet, most of us breathe shallowly, high in the chest, disconnected from its full power.

In feminine energy work, breath is the key to presence. It brings us back to our bodies, back to this moment, back to ourselves. The breath is also an emotional alchemist - it moves what has been stuck. It soothes what has been overwhelmed. It clears what no longer serves.

Deep belly breathing activates the parasympathetic nervous system, inviting rest, digestion, and repair. It also connects the heart and womb through a wave of movement that flows through the body. When we breathe deeply and intentionally, we remember that life itself is a rhythm of giving and receiving.

There are many breath practices in spiritual traditions, but the simplest are often the most powerful. Try inhaling slowly through your nose, feeling your belly expand, and exhaling gently through your mouth with a sigh. Repeat this for several minutes, allowing your body to soften. Notice what shifts.

Breath can also be used ceremonially. Before beginning a ritual, take three conscious breaths to center yourself. When releasing emotion, use a deeper exhale. When calling in something new, breathe it into your belly as if planting a seed. Your breath becomes your wand - directing energy, setting intention, weaving reality.

The breath is the original rhythm. It teaches us to receive and release. To fill and to empty. To be still and to flow. It is available to us at every moment, reminding us that no matter how far we drift, we can always come back - with one breath.

Closing Invitation

The breasts, belly, and breath form a trinity of feminine power. They are not separate parts, but interconnected centers that speak to one another through sensation, rhythm, and intuition. When we bring awareness to these areas, we awaken the body temple - not as an object to perfect, but as a sacred space to inhabit.

Touch your breasts with love. Hold your belly with reverence. Breathe like your life is sacred - because it is.

You do not need to look elsewhere for wisdom. It is here, in the rising of your chest, the fullness of your belly, the whisper of your breath.

The feminine lives in your body. And she is ready to be felt.

Chapter 8: The Voice as Vibration: Chanting, Storytelling, and Spoken Blessing

The voice is more than sound. It is vibration, frequency, and power in motion. It is the way energy leaves the inner world and enters the outer one. Through our voices, we express truth, offer healing, share wisdom, and cast intention into form. The feminine voice has long been silenced, mocked, or suppressed - not because it lacked power, but because it carried too much. Too much truth. Too much emotion. Too much knowing. But the ancient feminine was never voiceless. She sang the cosmos into being. She whispered blessings to rivers. She told stories by firelight. This chapter invites you to remember your voice not as a tool of performance, but as a sacred vessel. A bridge between the unseen and the seen. Your voice is not just what you say - it is who you are when you say it.

Chanting and the Power of Sound

In nearly every spiritual tradition, chanting and vocalization have been used to alter consciousness, create healing, and align with the divine. The sound of the voice carries vibration, and vibration shifts energy. Feminine wisdom has always included this awareness. Long before recorded music, women used their voices in circle, in ceremony, in birth, in grief, and in prayer.

Chanting activates the body. It vibrates the cells, massages the organs, and calms the mind. When we vocalize certain syllables or mantras, we are tuning the body like an instrument. This is not about singing "well" - it's about using sound with intention. The voice, when directed into the body with awareness, becomes medicine.

A simple and ancient sound used in feminine energy work is the "AH" sound. This open vowel is linked to the heart, the womb, and the breath. It opens the chest, softens the jaw, and grounds the voice. Chanting "AH" for several minutes each day can reconnect you to your body and clear energetic stagnation. The sound doesn't need to be loud. It needs to be felt.

Another powerful chant is "OM" - the primordial sound of creation in many traditions. When chanted slowly, it moves through the crown, throat, and heart, harmonizing the upper energy centers. It reminds us that our voice is not just ours - it is connected to something greater.

You might begin your own vocal practice by humming. Humming is a gentle, non-threatening way to begin reclaiming the voice. It soothes the nervous system, awakens the vagus nerve, and softens the chest. Let yourself hum when you're cooking, walking, bathing. Let your voice return to you without judgment.

Chanting in circle, especially with other women, can be profoundly healing. The resonance of multiple voices creates a field of coherence. This is one of the reasons why singing together was part of ancient rituals - it weaves community, balances the individual, and brings spirit into sound.

The Feminine Art of Storytelling

Women have always been the carriers of story. Long before books or scripts, stories were passed down through the breath, through grandmothers and mothers, through myth and memory. Storytelling was not entertainment - it was encoding. A way to teach wisdom, survival, love, grief, and spiritual law.

The feminine storytelling tradition is nonlinear. It spirals, weaves, remembers. It includes silence and gesture. It moves through emotion, not just logic. It is embodied, felt, alive. The storyteller is not only a narrator - she is a vessel. When she speaks, she channels a thread of something older than herself.

To reclaim storytelling as a feminine practice is to honor your voice as a vessel for lineage, insight, and transformation. Your stories matter - not just the polished ones, but the messy ones. The painful ones. The moments of grace that have no resolution. The raw truths you thought no one would understand.

Every time you speak your story with presence, you deconstruct shame. You show others what healing can look like. You make the invisible visible. And you remember that your voice is a thread in the great tapestry of humanity.

You don't have to be a performer to tell stories. You simply need to tell the truth. Begin by speaking aloud to yourself. Speak to your own heart, or to the trees, or to the sky. Let your voice carry your memories. Notice how it feels to say something out loud instead of just thinking it. Voice gives shape to emotion. Story gives context to experience.

If you feel fear about sharing your voice, that fear is likely ancestral. Many women were punished, exiled, or killed for speaking truth. That memory lives in the bones. But every time you tell your story - especially the one you were told not to tell - you undo a thread of that silencing.

You also activate healing for those who cannot yet speak. You become a lighthouse.

Spoken Blessing and the Energetics of Intention

Words shape reality. The vibration of speech is one of the fastest ways to direct energy. This is why prayer, affirmation, and blessing are such powerful spiritual technologies. They focus the mind, activate the heart, and send intention into the field.

Blessing is not just a religious act - it is a feminine one. It is the choice to infuse the ordinary with sacred energy. When you speak blessings - over food, over your body, over your home, over your day - you elevate the vibration of what you touch. You turn the mundane into ritual.

Blessings don't have to be formal. They can be whispered, sung, or spoken with a smile. They can be as simple as, "May this nourish me," or "Thank you, body, for carrying me," or "Let this home be a sanctuary." These small acts of spoken love accumulate. They create resonance.

One ancient practice is morning blessing. Upon waking, place your hand on your heart and say a blessing aloud. It can be your own words, or something simple like, "I bless this day. I bless this breath. I bless this body." Notice how this shifts your energy. It's not about performance - it's about presence.

Another practice is the water blessing. Speak to your glass of water before drinking it. Offer it a word, an intention, a vibration. Water holds memory. When we speak love into water, and then drink it, we are literally imprinting our bodies with that vibration.

Blessing others with your voice is equally powerful. Whether spoken aloud or silently, sending someone a blessing of peace, healing, or strength is an act of feminine leadership. It is influence without control. It is love without agenda. It is transmission through frequency.

Your voice carries energy. Use it not only to express, but to bless. Not only to speak, but to transmit. When you do, your life becomes a prayer in motion.

Closing Invitation

Your voice is not small. It is not too much. It is not meant to fit into someone else's comfort zone. Your voice is vibration - it is energy, emotion, memory, and medicine. It is your birthright and your tool of reclamation.

Let yourself chant. Let yourself hum. Let yourself tell stories that are still trembling on your tongue. Let yourself bless your life out loud.

You do not need permission to speak your truth.

You only need to remember that your voice is already sacred.

Speak, not to be heard - but to be free.

PART III: ANCESTRAL RITUALS & ACTIVATIONS

Chapter 9: The Blessing Bowl Ceremony: An Old Ritual for Releasing and Receiving

There are moments in life when something inside us longs to be released - a belief, a pattern, a wound we've been carrying for too long. And there are moments, too, when we are ready to call something new into our lives: a deeper truth, a clearer path, an answered prayer. The ancient feminine traditions understood that true transformation requires ritual. Not performance, but presence. Not spectacle, but intention. The Blessing Bowl Ceremony is a simple but profound practice that brings form to this invisible process. It is a container for letting go and calling in. It reminds us that we do not need to wait for life to change us - we can participate in the alchemy.

The Bowl as Sacred Vessel

Across cultures and spiritual paths, the bowl appears as a sacred object. It is the womb in physical form: open, curved, receptive. Bowls have held offerings to deities, ashes of ancestors, sacred waters, and prayers whispered in silence. They are both practical and mystical. In the Blessing Bowl Ceremony, the bowl becomes a symbol of your own readiness to participate in your healing. It becomes the container for your release and your invitation. You don't need an ornate vessel to begin. A ceramic dish, a handmade clay bowl, or even a large seashell can become sacred when you approach it with intention. What matters most is the energy you bring to it. Before beginning your ceremony, spend a moment holding your bowl in your hands. Close your eyes. Feel its shape, its weight. Ask it silently to become your ally in this ritual. The bowl holds space for what you're ready to let go of. It holds space for what you're ready to receive. Like the womb, it is nonjudgmental. It does not rush or resist. It welcomes.

Many people choose to fill their bowl with water, symbolizing fluidity, emotional depth, and purification. Water is a conductor of energy and has been used in spiritual practices for millennia. When combined with your words and your intention, the water in your bowl becomes a mirror, a healer, and a witness. The Blessing Bowl reminds us that change doesn't have to be dramatic to be real. Sometimes the deepest shifts happen when we give our inner life a shape, a gesture, a form.

Ritual for Release: Pouring Out the Old

To release something is to make space for something else. But letting go is not always easy, especially when what we are releasing has defined us - an old role, an outdated belief, a scar we've grown used to touching. The first half of the Blessing Bowl Ceremony is about honoring what has been and gently inviting it to leave.

To begin, find a quiet space. Light a candle if you like. Place your bowl in front of you, filled with clean water. Sit with it. Breathe deeply. Then, take a piece of paper and write down what you are ready to release. This could be one thing or many. Be specific, honest, and kind. Hold the paper in your hands and read it aloud. Speak it into the water. This is not about drama - it is about intimacy. You are acknowledging what has been. You are naming what no longer serves you.

Then, tear the paper into small pieces and place them into the water. As they dissolve or float, visualize the energy of those words leaving your body, your mind, your field. Say something simple, like: "I release this now. I thank it for what it taught me. I am ready to let it go."

You may cry. You may feel nothing at first. You may feel a deep breath move through your belly. Trust the process. This ritual is not a performance - it is a conversation between you and the unseen.

Some people choose to add a pinch of salt to the water after the release, symbolizing purification. Others might stir the water with their fingers, feeling the current shift. Do what feels natural to you. This is your ceremony.

When you are ready, dispose of the water respectfully - into the Earth, down the drain with intention, or beneath a tree. Thank it. You have now cleared a space within you.

Ritual for Receiving: Inviting the New

Once we release, we must invite. Nature abhors a vacuum, and the soul, too, longs to be filled - with truth, beauty, peace, love. The second half of the Blessing Bowl Ceremony is about calling in what your heart desires. It is about choosing to receive not through force, but through alignment.

Clean your bowl and refil it with fresh water. Sit before it once again. This time, take another piece of paper and write down what you are ready to receive. It could be a quality - like courage or joy - or a specific vision, like a new home, a creative breakthrough, a healed relationship.

Speak these desires into the water. Let your voice carry not only the words, but the emotion behind them. Let yourself feel the longing, the hope, the clarity. As you speak, imagine that the water is being charged with your intention. That it is holding your prayer in its molecules.

Place your hands over the bowl and breathe deeply. Say aloud, "I am ready to receive. I welcome this into my life. I trust in divine timing. I open to the highest good." Some people place a flower, a crystal, or a few drops of essential oil into the water to symbolize beauty and presence. Others hold the bowl close to their heart and sit in meditation, letting the energy of their desire fill their body.

You may wish to anoint your forehead, heart, and belly with a few drops of the water - bringing the blessing into your body. Or you may pour the water into the soil as an offering to the Earth, planting your prayer. The key is not in the specific steps, but in your sincerity. This is about participation. You are choosing to align your energy with what you long for. You are meeting life halfway.

Closing Invitation

The Blessing Bowl Ceremony is a feminine ritual because it honors both release and reception. It does not force or manipulate. You can perform this ceremony monthly, with the new moon, or whenever you feel a transition in your life. You can do it alone, or in circle.

You are not passive in your healing. You are a co-creator. A vessel. A participant in the mystery.

Let the bowl be your mirror. Let the water carry your truth.

Let the ritual become your prayer. You are ready to release.

You are ready to receive. And the sacred is ready to meet you.

Chapter 10: Earth Offerings & Elemental Prayer: Working with Water, Fire, Air, and Earth

The feminine has always been elemental. She does not live only in temples or books - she breathes in rivers, burns in hearths, dances in winds, and rests in soil. The elements are not abstract forces. They are alive, present, and deeply connected to our bodies and spirits. Earth, water, fire, and air have been called upon by ancient cultures across the world as both allies and teachers. They represent the building blocks of life and the pathways of sacred connection. Offering to the elements is not about dogma or superstition - it is about relationship. It is about remembering that we are part of the living world, not separate from it. And that we can enter into communion with nature not only through observation, but through reverence. This chapter invites you into the ancient practice of earth offerings and elemental prayer - a way of grounding your intentions, honoring the land, and weaving your life back into the web of all that is.

Earth: Anchoring, Belonging, and Physical Prayer

The element of Earth is the body of the world. It is stone and root, mountain and bone. Earth is slow, stable, and supportive. It teaches us to ground, to hold, to become. In feminine wisdom traditions, Earth is associated with the mother - the provider, the sustainer, the fertile one. To connect with the Earth is to remember our belonging, to sink out of the mind and into the body, to come home to ourselves.

Earth offerings are a gesture of gratitude and respect. They are a way of saying: I see you. I honor you. I return what has been taken. These offerings can be as simple as placing flowers at the base of a tree, burying a stone with your prayer, or leaving a piece of fruit in a wild place. What matters is not the object, but the energy.

When you make an earth offering, pause. Place your hands on the ground. Speak from your heart. Say thank you for the breath in your lungs, the food in your belly, the gravity that holds you. Ask permission. Listen. The Earth may not speak in words, but she responds in feeling. You may feel a softening, a presence, a return.

You can also anchor your intentions into the earth. Write a prayer or vision on a piece of paper, fold it, and bury it under a rock or tree. Let it decompose and integrate. This is not just symbolic - it's energetic. The Earth knows how to hold what we give her.

Walking barefoot, lying on the ground, gardening with intention - these are all ways of praying with your body. Earth invites you to slow down, to trust the process, to remember that healing happens over time, like seeds becoming roots.

Water: Emotion, Intuition, and Fluid Prayer

Water is the element of emotion, intuition, memory, and flow. It cleanses, nourishes, carries, and transforms. In the feminine lineage, water is deeply sacred. It is the realm of the womb, the moon, the tides, the tears. To work with water is to soften. To open. To feel.

Water offerings are ancient. In countless cultures, libations - liquid offerings - have been poured to the spirits, ancestors, and gods. These could be water, wine, milk, or herbal infusions. The act of pouring is symbolic of surrender, generosity, and the desire to connect. You pour what you love to what you love.

You can offer water to a stream, a plant, or a bowl on your altar. You might infuse it with flowers, speak your prayer into it, and then return it to the Earth. Rainwater is especially powerful, as it comes directly from the sky, carrying the charge of the atmosphere.

One deeply feminine practice is to bless your own tears. Instead of wiping them away quickly, pause and touch them with reverence. Let them fall onto the Earth or into your bowl. Say, "These are sacred. These are my offerings." In doing so, you reclaim your emotional expression as holy.

Water also mirrors us. Sit by a body of water - river, lake, ocean, even a small pond - and speak your heart aloud. Water holds memory. It will receive you without judgment. You can also write your emotions onto paper, float it on water, and let it be carried away.

Bathing can become ritual when approached with intention. Add herbs, salt, or flowers to your bath. Set a theme or prayer - release, renewal, clarity - and let the water hold you. As you drain the bath, visualize your old stories washing away. This is water as priestess, healer, and midwife.

Fire: Transformation, Passion, and Devotional Flame

Fire is the element of transformation, passion, creativity, and spiritual ignition. It is both destructive and illuminating. It burns away what is false and lights the path forward. In feminine rites, fire has been used to mark thresholds, burn offerings, and activate will. It is the wild, the fierce, the awake.

To make a fire offering, you don't need a bonfire or ceremonial space. A candle is enough. Write what you are ready to release - fear, anger, a limiting belief - and burn it in a safe container. Watch the flames consume it. Let the smoke rise as a prayer. Fire does not ask for perfection - it asks for presence.

You can also offer to fire what you love. Sacred herbs like rosemary, sage, lavender, or bay leaves can be burned slowly, each one representing a quality you wish to embody - peace, strength, clarity. This is not about destruction, but transmutation. Fire changes form but never erases essence.

Cooking can become a fire ritual when done with love. Stir your soup with a prayer. Bake your bread with gratitude. Light a flame before preparing food and dedicate the meal to something greater - healing, joy, communion. In this way, fire becomes part of daily devotion.

The hearth has long been a symbol of feminine power - the center of warmth, life, and storytelling. Lighting a fire in your home (even a candle) and sitting before it in stillness can remind you of the fire within. That you, too, are both heat and light.

Air: Breath, Thought, and Invisible Communion

Air is the element of breath, thought, spirit, and the invisible realms. It is the whisper of intuition, the clarity of the mind, the messenger between worlds. Air moves freely - it cannot be held, only felt. It is the wind in your hair, the space between words, the inhale before a song.

To offer to air is to speak, to sing, to exhale. Spoken prayer is an air ritual. So is chanting, sighing, and even laughter. The air carries your voice to the unseen. When you speak your truth aloud under the open sky, it does not vanish - it travels.

You can write a blessing or prayer and tie it to a tree branch, allowing the wind to carry it. You can burn sacred herbs and let the smoke rise. You can light incense as a way to mark space, calling spirit into presence. These are all invitations to the air - to join you, to witness, to hold.

Breathwork is a direct communion with this element. The more consciously we breathe, the more attuned we become to the unseen parts of ourselves. Inhale trust, exhale resistance. Inhale vision, exhale doubt. Let your breath become the bridge.

Dreams are also of the air realm. Keep a notebook near your bed and record them. Pay attention to the messages that come on the wind -

sudden insights, a feather falling, a change in the breeze. The feminine lives in these subtle cues. She moves through the air like a whisper waiting to be heard.

Closing Invitation

Working with the elements is not a technique - it is a relationship. The Earth is not a symbol. She is a being. Water is not a metaphor. She is alive. Fire is not just heat. It is a spirit. Air is not just wind. It is breath.

When you make offerings, you are not begging or performing. You are conversing. You are remembering that you are part of a living world that responds to reverence.

Let your prayers be carried by the wind.

Let your grief be held by water.

Let your vision be lit by fire.

Let your body be rooted in Earth.

You are not separate from nature.

You are nature, remembering herself.

Chapter 11: Feminine Circle Magic: Why Women Gathered - And How We Can Again

There is a quiet power in a circle. No head. No hierarchy. Just presence. In ancient times, the feminine gathered not in rows, not in pyramids of power, but in circles. Around fires, around altars, around each other. The circle was not just a shape - it was a consciousness. It represented equality, unity, and the sacred container that could hold grief, joy, wisdom, blood, birth, and death. It was where women came to be seen, to be held, to be reminded of who they were when the world tried to make them forget. Though the circle may have faded from our modern structures, it has never disappeared. It lives in our longing for community, for shared ritual, for spaces where we do not have to perform. This chapter explores the ancient practice of feminine circle magic, why it matters now more than ever, and how we can gather again - with intention, with reverence, and with realness.

The Ancient Roots of Women's Circles

Long before written history, women gathered in ritual. Archaeological evidence points to communal spaces dedicated to goddess worship, lunar ceremonies, seasonal rites, and the transitions of womanhood. These gatherings were not passive or ornamental - they were central to the spiritual and social fabric of early cultures. The feminine circle was where knowledge was passed down, where the mysteries were kept, where the rhythms of life were honored.

In matrilineal and Indigenous cultures, circles served as spaces of initiation, healing, and governance. They were intergenerational, weaving together elders, mothers, maidens, and children. Women gathered to tend the fire, prepare food, tell stories, share dreams, and witness one another through birth, menstruation, pregnancy, menopause, and mourning. The cycle of life was not something to endure alone - it was something to move through together.

The circle also functioned as a ceremonial space. Full moon rituals, solstice gatherings, and rites of passage were often held in circular form, symbolizing the never-ending flow of life, death, and rebirth. Songs were sung in harmony. Prayers were spoken aloud. Silence was honored. There was no performance, no spotlight. Just presence.

With the rise of patriarchal religion, colonization, and institutional systems, many of these gatherings were labeled dangerous or heretical. Women were discouraged - or outright forbidden - from meeting in private or practicing spiritual rites outside of sanctioned doctrine. The result was a silencing not just of the feminine voice, but of the feminine collective body.

But the circle never truly disappeared. It went underground. It hid in sewing circles, kitchen tables, birth rooms, and whispered prayers. And now, it is rising again - not as a nostalgic return, but as a necessary revolution of remembrance.

The Medicine of Being Witnessed

In a culture that rewards individuality and competition, we often forget how vital it is to be witnessed. To be truly seen without judgment, without advice, without interruption. The feminine circle offers this medicine. It creates a field where the masks can fall, the defenses can soften, and the truth can emerge - raw, radiant, and real.

To be witnessed is not the same as being observed. Observation comes from the outside. Witnessing is sacred. It says, "I see you. I hold space for you. I do not need to fix or change you. I trust your process." In a circle, each woman becomes a mirror - not to distort, but to reflect the beauty and complexity of the other.

One of the most powerful practices in circle is the simple act of sharing. A woman speaks her truth - a joy, a grief, a story, a breakthrough - and the others listen. No cross-talk, no unsolicited advice, just deep presence. This practice is rooted in the belief that each person has an inner wisdom that knows the way forward, and that being heard is often what activates it.

When we are witnessed in this way, something alchemical happens. The shame dissolves. The armor softens. The wound finds air and begins to heal. We realize we are not alone in our struggle, nor isolated in our joy. The circle reminds us that we are part of something larger than ourselves.

This kind of witnessing also cultivates deep empathy. As we listen to the stories of others, we learn to hold space not just for them, but for the parts of ourselves we may have silenced. We develop the capacity to feel with, not just for. And this is the root of all true feminine leadership - not dominance, but resonance.

Creating and Holding Modern-Day Circles

You do not need to be a priestess, facilitator, or expert to gather a circle. You only need the desire to create sacred space. The feminine circle is not about perfection - it is about presence. Whether you gather three women or thirty, indoors or outdoors, monthly or spontaneously, what matters is your intention.

Begin by creating a clear container. This means setting the energetic tone and boundaries of the space. Let those who gather know that the circle is a space of confidentiality, respect, and deep listening. You might open the space with a few breaths, a short meditation, or a shared candle lighting.

Seating in a circle - on cushions, chairs, or the ground - creates a sense of equality. There is no head of the table, no podium. Everyone is a vital part of the whole. You may choose to have a talking piece - an object that is held when someone is speaking - to support presence and flow.

Each gathering can have a theme or be open-ended. You might center the circle around the new or full moon, a seasonal transition, a collective intention, or a shared reading. The circle can include sharing, journaling, gentle movement, ritual, song, silence, or whatever arises organically. The goal is not to entertain - it is to attune.

Holding space means trusting the intelligence of the group. Sometimes there will be tears. Sometimes laughter. Sometimes long pauses. All of it belongs. Your role as circle holder is not to control the experience, but to protect the sacredness of it.

When the circle is complete, it's important to close it intentionally. This could be with a prayer, a chant, a group breath, or a moment of silence. Closing the circle seals the energy and honors the time you've spent together. It's also a signal to the psyche that something meaningful has occurred.

Remember: this is not about doing it "right." It's about remembering how to gather again in a world that has forgotten. It's about creating places where the feminine can speak, listen, cry, laugh, and be.

Closing Invitation

The circle is more than a shape - it is a space of return. To your voice. To your body. To your truth. And to others who are walking the same spiral path.

Gathering in circle is not a trend. It is a remembering. Of how we used to meet. Of how we used to heal. Of how we used to lead.

The magic of the feminine does not live in isolation. It lives in community. In shared ritual. In deep listening. In sacred space that honors the whole of who we are.

Whether you join a circle or create your own, know this: every time women gather in love and presence, the world shifts. The field changes. The forgotten becomes visible.

And the sacred becomes real again.

Let the circle hold you.

Let it see you.

Let it remind you: you are never alone.

Chapter 12: The Rite of Reclamation: A Guided Solo Ritual for Returning to Your Feminine Essence

There comes a time when remembering is no longer enough. When reading, reflecting, and understanding are no longer sufficient. The soul begins to call for embodiment - for a ritual, an act, a moment in which we step fully into ourselves and say: I return. I remember. I reclaim. Feminine wisdom is not something we access only through study - it is something we awaken through experience. The Rite of Reclamation is a solo ritual, a sacred encounter between you and your essence. It is a ceremony of return, of reconnection, and of commitment to your deepest truth. This is not about performing for others or seeking validation. It is about standing in your own sacred space and choosing yourself as holy. Reclamation is not loud, but it is powerful. It happens when we no longer abandon who we are. It begins in silence, is shaped by intention, and becomes a portal to the feminine within.

Preparing the Sacred Space

Before you begin, allow yourself the time and space to enter ritual without rush. Choose a time when you won't be interrupted. Turn off your phone, dim the lights, and create an environment that feels safe, sacred, and beautiful. This is your temple space, and it should reflect care and reverence.

Select items that represent the four elements to anchor the space energetically. A candle for fire, a bowl of water for water, a stone or flower for earth, and incense, feathers, or breath for air. These elemental symbols remind us that we are connected to the greater web of life, and that the feminine exists not just within, but all around us.

Consider also placing items on your altar or around your circle that have personal meaning - photos of ancestors, symbols of your journey, sacred texts, or anything that speaks to the energy of the feminine you wish to reclaim.

Dress in a way that feels intentional, even ceremonial. This could mean wearing white, flowing fabrics, a shawl, or simply being barefoot and bare-faced. What matters is how it feels to you - not how it looks.

Before beginning, take several deep breaths and place your hands on your heart or lower belly. Say aloud or silently: "I am here. I am ready. I enter this space in devotion to my truth."

This simple act of preparing with presence is itself a reclamation. It declares that your inner world is worth your time, attention, and love.

The Three Gates: Descent, Stillness, and Emergence

The Rite of Reclamation unfolds in three phases. Each is a symbolic gate you pass through - first, to descend into what has been forgotten; second, to meet the stillness of your true essence; and third, to emerge as one who remembers.

Begin the descent by lighting your candle and turning your gaze inward. Close your eyes and allow yourself to reflect on the places within where you have disconnected from your feminine essence. You might remember moments of silencing your intuition, shaming your body, denying your softness, or shrinking your light to make others comfortable.

Allow any emotions to arise - grief, anger, sadness, or even numbness. All of it is welcome. Speak aloud if you feel moved to, naming what you are leaving behind. You might say: "I release the belief that I must be small to be safe," or "I release the silence I was taught to keep."

As you do this, write down these old identities or beliefs on pieces of paper. One by one, place them in a bowl or dish. When complete, burn them safely or tear them apart, offering the ashes or scraps to the earth.

This is your descent - the release, the letting go, the sacred death of the false self.

Now enter the second gate: stillness. Blow out the candle and sit in darkness or low light. This is the womb space, the void, the place of potential before becoming. You are not broken. You are between.

Sit or lie down, eyes closed, hands on your body. Feel your breath. Listen to your heartbeat. Let go of all effort. In this stillness, ask: "Who am I without the stories?" Allow whatever arises to come without grasping. It may be silence. It may be a memory. It may be a vision. Receive it all as sacred.

You can remain here for minutes or longer. This is the heart of the ritual - the place where the noise of the world is replaced by the sound of your soul.

When you feel ready, move to the final gate: emergence. Light the candle again, signaling your return from the inner world with something reborn. Now take a moment to claim your truth.

Speak aloud affirmations of your reclamation. These can be your own words or inspired phrases such as:

- I reclaim my voice as sacred.
- I reclaim my body as worthy.
- I reclaim my softness as strength.
- I reclaim my intuition as guidance.
- I reclaim my presence as enough.

You may wish to anoint yourself with water, oil, or flower essence. Touch your forehead, your heart, your womb, your feet. Say aloud: "I return to myself. I honor who I am. I choose to walk as the woman I was always becoming."

This is the moment of embodiment - not just knowing who you are, but feeling it. Standing in it. Speaking it. Let it land in your cells, your bones, your breath.

Integrating the Ceremony into Daily Life

Rituals are beautiful portals - but their true power lies in how we integrate them into the everyday. After the Rite of Reclamation, you may feel tender, raw, inspired, or clear. Whatever you feel, give yourself space to land. Drink water. Rest. Journal what arose. Let your body catch up to your soul.

To continue the energy of the ritual, consider a daily or weekly practice that reminds you of your reclamation. This could be a morning breath practice, a short affirmation, a sacred object you wear or carry, or simply placing your hand on your heart and whispering, "I'm still here."

Let others see this new embodiment - through your boundaries, your self-love, your willingness to be soft and strong at once. Let your presence become the ritual. You are not performing your feminine. You are living it.

This reclamation is not a one-time event. It is a lifelong unfolding. There will be days when you forget, when old stories return, when you question the journey. That is normal. That is human. What matters is that you now have a place to return to - a ritual, a memory, a truth in your bones.

You have walked through the three gates. You have entered yourself. You have remembered that your power is not in how others perceive you, but in how fully you are willing to know yourself.

Let this be your vow: to never again leave yourself behind.

Let this be your beginning: to walk in beauty, anchored in the feminine essence that was never lost - only waiting.

You have reclaimed her.

And she is home.

PART IV: EMBODYING THE FEMININE BLESSINGS

Chapter 13: From Suppression to Sovereignty: Healing the Wound of Being "Too Much" or "Not Enough"

There is a wound many of us carry, passed down through generations, reinforced by culture, and often internalized before we even have words to name it. It is the wound of not being right as we are - too loud or too quiet, too wild or too passive, too emotional, too sensitive, too demanding, too much. Or its mirror twin: not enough. Not beautiful enough, not smart enough, not worthy enough, not feminine enough. This wound is not personal, though it feels deeply intimate. It is collective. It lives in the bodies of women and feminine beings across time and space. It has silenced, shrunk, hardened, and hidden us. But the feminine was never meant to fit a mold. She was meant to be free. This chapter is about remembering that sovereignty is your birthright. It's about healing the internalized suppression and stepping into your wholeness - not by becoming someone new, but by returning to who you were before the world told you to be smaller.

The Roots of Suppression

To understand how we heal, we must understand how we were hurt. Suppression didn't begin with a single event. It began with a system - a system that feared the feminine because it couldn't control her. In ancient times, the feminine was worshipped as a force of nature, mystery, and power. But as patriarchal structures took hold, that power was labeled dangerous, chaotic, and untrustworthy.

We were taught that emotion is weakness. That softness is vulnerability. That intuition is superstition. That beauty is a currency to be earned. Over time, we began to edit ourselves. We split off from parts of our own being. We learned to smile when we wanted to scream, to agree when we wanted to walk away, to be "nice" instead of true.

This suppression is often subtle. It shows up in the voice we lower so we're not called "shrill." In the ideas we don't share because we don't want to seem arrogant. In the clothing we change because someone else might be uncomfortable. It shows up in how we apologize for our existence, our needs, our brilliance.

And yet, even in the thick of suppression, there is always a spark of memory. A part of you that knows who you are. That remembers your fullness. That hungers for freedom. That is your sovereign self. She may be buried, quiet, forgotten - but she has never left you. She is waiting for your return.

The Journey of Healing and Remembering

The journey from suppression to sovereignty is not linear. It is a spiral. A deepening. A cycle of remembering and forgetting, shedding and reclaiming. It begins with awareness - with noticing the places where you've silenced yourself, where you've adopted masks, where you've abandoned your truth to belong.

Start by listening to the voice in your head when you make a decision. Does it say, "What will they think?" before it says, "What do I want?" Does it tell you to be careful, to be small, to not rock the boat? This voice is not your enemy - it is your protector. It learned to keep you safe in a world that punished feminine expression. But it does not have to lead anymore.

Practice honoring your "too much." What are the parts of you you've been told to tone down? Your anger? Your sensuality? Your ambition? Your intensity? These are not flaws - they are flames. Let yourself feel them. Let them move through your body. Dance them. Write them. Speak them. Give them space.

At the same time, hold compassion for your "not enough." The places where you still doubt your worth, where you feel behind, where shame lives. These tender parts don't need to be fixed - they need to be held. Sovereignty isn't about being fearless. It's about being loving toward your fears.

One powerful practice is mirror work. Stand before a mirror, look into your own eyes, and speak to yourself with kindness. Say what you've never been told. "You are enough." "You are safe to be seen." "Your voice matters." This may feel strange at first - but over time, it rewires the inner dialogue. It creates new pathways of self-connection.

Community is also key. We cannot reclaim ourselves in isolation. Find people who reflect your truth back to you, who celebrate your too-muchness and see your enoughness. Circles, sisters, coaches, or simply friends who honor your path - these are sacred mirrors.

Most importantly, sovereignty is not about perfection. It is about presence. It is about showing up in your wholeness, knowing you are allowed to be messy, radiant, contradictory, and real. You are allowed to take up space. You are allowed to change your mind. You are allowed to lead, cry, rest, roar, and rise.

Sovereignty in Action: Living Unapologetically

Once you begin to reclaim your feminine essence, the question becomes: How do I live this truth in the world? How do I embody sovereignty not just in ritual, but in daily life?

It begins with choice. Sovereignty means choosing from your center, not from fear or people-pleasing. It means pausing before saying yes, checking in with your body before committing, and honoring your intuition even when it goes against logic or external approval.

Boundaries are essential. Not as walls, but as containers. A sovereign woman knows that saying no is a sacred act. That her energy is precious. That she does not owe anyone access to her time, body, or emotional labor. Boundaries are not selfish - they are self-honoring. And they create the conditions in which your true self can thrive.

Voice is another portal. Speak your truth, even when your voice shakes. Especially when your voice shakes. Use your voice to express, not to perform. To connect, not to control. Whether in conversation, creation, or leadership, your voice is your wand. It casts the spell of your becoming.

And then, there is pleasure. A sovereign woman is not ruled by external validation - she is nourished from within. She makes space for pleasure not as reward, but as a right. This doesn't mean indulgence without awareness - it means presence with what brings life. Pleasure might be rest, creativity, sensuality, or simply stillness. It is the art of being with what delights your soul.

Finally, sovereignty is about responsibility. Not in the heavy, guilt-laden sense - but in the empowered sense of owning your life. You are not a victim of your past, your conditioning, or your culture. You are the author of your story now. And each day, you get to choose: Will I live in suppression? Or will I live in remembrance?

You won't always get it right. You'll fall back into old patterns. That's okay. What matters is that you return. Again and again. That you choose yourself. That you stand in your truth - not because you have something to prove, but because you have something to live.

Closing Invitation

Suppression may have shaped your past, but it does not have to define your future. You are not too much. You are not not enough. You are exactly as vast, as wild, as deep, and as radiant as you were meant to be.

Sovereignty is not something you earn. It is something you remember.

And when you remember, you become dangerous to all that would silence you - and holy to all that would walk beside you.

Stand tall. Speak truth. Take up space. Love yourself back to wholeness.

This is your return. This is your power. This is your feminine, free.

Chapter 14: Living in Ceremony: Everyday Acts as Sacred Gestures

Ceremony is often imagined as something elaborate - candles lit in sacred temples, chants rising into the air, robes, rituals, and solemn silence. But at its essence, ceremony is simply the act of bringing intention into form. It is a way of living in which nothing is too small to matter. For the ancient feminine, life itself was a ceremony. Waking, eating, bleeding, bathing, working, resting - each act was a chance to connect with the divine. The separation between sacred and mundane did not exist. What we have lost in modern life is not just access to rituals, but the understanding that we are meant to live inside of them. This chapter is a gentle reminder and a powerful invitation: you do not have to wait for the new moon or a retreat or a crisis to step into sacredness. You can live your life as ceremony, right now, through the smallest acts done with presence.

The Power of Intention in the Everyday

The difference between routine and ritual is intention. A cup of tea can be a habit or it can be a prayer. A walk can be a mindless escape or a sacred dialogue with the earth. Living in ceremony is not about doing different things - it is about doing the same things differently, with more presence, more heart, more awareness.

Begin by choosing one ordinary act in your daily life to infuse with intention. This could be your morning shower, the way you prepare your food, or how you enter your workspace. Before you begin, pause. Take a breath. Acknowledge what you are about to do. Say silently, "This is sacred." Then move with awareness. That's it. You've created a ceremony.

When we slow down enough to be present, everything becomes a portal. Washing dishes becomes an act of cleansing more than just plates. Brushing your hair becomes a conversation with your body. Folding laundry becomes a meditation in gratitude. These are not chores - they are chances to connect with the now, to return to the self.

Intention also brings clarity to our energy. When we act unconsciously, we often move through life fragmented, distracted, or reactive. But when we bring sacredness into the moment, we align. We begin to notice how we feel, what we need, what we're really longing for. Ceremony is not about adding more - it's about doing less, more fully.

You can also use intention to mark thresholds. Lighting a candle at the start of the day. Placing a hand on your heart before a conversation. Offering a breath before beginning a project. These small moments ground us, guide us, and remind us that we are participants in our lives, not just passive observers.

Creating Personal Rituals That Matter

While living in ceremony includes daily acts, it also involves creating rituals that reflect who you are and what you value. Personal rituals are like spiritual signatures - they are uniquely yours. They don't have to follow any rule or tradition unless it speaks to your soul. They are expressions of your truth, shaped in time and space.

To create your own ritual, begin by asking: What do I want to honor? What do I want to release, receive, or remember? From there, build a structure that feels natural. Rituals often include a beginning, a middle, and a closing - just like a story.

The beginning might involve setting the space. Light a candle, burn incense, or play music that opens your heart. You might speak an invocation, such as "I open this space to love and truth," or "May this be a space of clarity and peace."

The middle is the core of your ritual. This could be writing and burning a letter, dancing to release energy, journaling, meditating, or creating something with your hands. Let this part reflect your intention. If you are grieving, let yourself cry. If you are celebrating, let yourself sing. Ritual does not have to be solemn. Joy is sacred, too.

The closing is your way of sealing the energy. Blow out the candle. Offer thanks. Take a breath. Touch the earth. Drink water. Do something that marks the return from the inner space to the outer world. Integration is just as important as invocation.

Over time, you might develop rituals for key moments in your life - new beginnings, full moon releases, creative initiations, or healing closures. You might mark your menstrual cycle with a monthly ceremony or create a morning ritual to anchor your day.

The most powerful rituals are not always the most complex. They are the ones you return to because they bring you home to yourself. Ritual becomes rhythm, and rhythm becomes a way of living in connection with your own soul.

Sacred Objects and Anchors of Devotion

Living in ceremony is not just about what you do - it's also about what surrounds you. Sacred objects can act as anchors, reminders, and vessels for your energy and intention. These can be crystals, flowers, candles, journals, art, jewelry, or anything that feels meaningful to you.

Create a small altar in your home. It doesn't have to be large or elaborate. A shelf, a corner of a table, or even a window sill can become a space of devotion. Place items on it that reflect your spiritual path - symbols of the elements, photos of ancestors, affirmations, or seasonal tokens from nature.

Visit your altar regularly. Not as a duty, but as a return. Sit in front of it in silence. Light a candle. Speak a truth. Make an offering. This practice is not about religion - it's about remembering. The altar becomes a mirror, reflecting back your own sacredness.

You can also carry sacredness with you. Wear a necklace with a stone that grounds you. Carry a small object in your pocket that reminds you of your intention. Use essential oils, talismans, or tattoos that hold symbolic meaning. These are not accessories - they are tools for embodiment.

Sacredness lives in the tangible. When we infuse physical space with spiritual energy, we create a field of coherence. Our homes become sanctuaries. Our bodies become temples. Our lives become altars.

The feminine is deeply sensorial. She feels through touch, scent, sight, and sound. Surround yourself with beauty, not as decoration, but as devotion. Flowers on your table. Music that stirs your heart. Fabrics that feel like love on your skin. These are all gestures of sacred living.

Closing Invitation

Living in ceremony is not about becoming someone else - it's about remembering who you are beneath the noise. It's about bringing the sacred back to the center of your life, not as a concept, but as a daily experience.

You do not need a special occasion to honor your life. Waking up is ceremony. Feeding your body is ceremony. Saying "thank you" is ceremony. Listening to your own breath is ceremony.

You are the priestess. Your life is the temple.

Bring intention to your steps. Let beauty touch your eyes. Let presence shape your moments. Let reverence be your rhythm.

This is the feminine path: rooted in the Earth, open to the sky, and alive in the now.

Let each act be a blessing.

Let each breath be a prayer.

Let your life be the ceremony.

Chapter 15: The Feminine in Relationship: Boundaries, Magnetism, and Emotional Intimacy

The feminine is not only a solitary force of introspection and self-discovery - she is also relational. She exists in how we connect, how we love, how we receive and respond to others. Relationship is where the feminine often meets her deepest joys and her deepest wounds. It is where she is asked to stay open even when she is afraid, to be soft without losing herself, to give without self-abandonment. For centuries, feminine energy in relationship has been shaped by distorted models - submission without sovereignty, caretaking without reciprocity, giving without receiving. But the true feminine in relationship is neither passive nor dominant; she is magnetic, expressive, emotionally wise, and deeply attuned to her inner truth. This chapter is about reclaiming how we relate from a place of wholeness. Whether you are in romantic partnership, deep friendship, or seeking community, these principles apply. Because the way we show up in relationship reveals what we believe about ourselves - and also creates the field where the sacred feminine can be seen, shared, and sustained.

Boundaries as Sacred Containers

One of the most misunderstood aspects of feminine energy is the role of boundaries. Many people associate the feminine with openness, receptivity, and unconditional love. While this is true, it is only half the picture. The other half is discernment, containment, and sovereignty. Without boundaries, receptivity becomes depletion. Without discernment, connection becomes entanglement. The healthy feminine is open-hearted - but not porous.

A boundary is not a wall; it is a sacred container. It defines where you begin and where you end. It protects your time, your energy, your body, and your emotional well-being. It allows you to give from fullness, not obligation. When you set a boundary, you are not pushing others away - you are inviting in a relationship based on truth, clarity, and mutual respect.

For many women, boundaries have been difficult to assert. We have been conditioned to please, to avoid conflict, to prioritize harmony at our own expense. But the path of the awakened feminine involves reclaiming the right to say no. To listen to the body's signals. To honor the gut feeling that something is off. Every time you hold a boundary, you reinforce to yourself: I am worthy of care. I do not have to abandon myself to be loved.

Start by tuning into where your energy contracts around others. Do you feel drained after certain conversations? Do you say yes when you mean no? These are signs that a boundary is needed. Boundaries do not always need to be declared with confrontation - they can be held with quiet clarity. Leaving a conversation early. Taking space. Saying, "Let me think about that and get back to you."

The most magnetic people are not the ones who give endlessly - they are the ones who know where they end and where others begin. Boundaries create trust, both within and without. They make your yes meaningful because it comes from freedom, not fear.

The Power of Feminine Magnetism

Feminine energy in relationship does not chase - it attracts. This is the principle of magnetism: the power to draw toward you what is aligned, without force, manipulation, or self-sacrifice. True magnetism comes from embodiment. From being rooted in your body, your truth, your pleasure, your presence. When you are full within yourself, you naturally become magnetic. You become a field that others want to enter - not because you are performing, but because you are radiating.

In contrast to the cultural narrative that says we must constantly strive, prove, or earn love, feminine magnetism teaches that our presence is enough. That when we are centered in our joy, our softness, our clarity, we create a resonance that calls forth those who are ready to meet us.

This does not mean you never take action or express desire. It means that your action arises from alignment, not anxiety. That your desire is shared vulnerably, not as a strategy to be chosen. Feminine magnetism is not about seduction in the superficial sense - it is about resonance. When you are true to yourself, you attract what is true.

Practices to cultivate magnetism include pleasure rituals, dance, self-anointing, mirror work, and creative expression. Anything that brings you alive in your body will increase your magnetic field. Because magnetism is not about doing more - it's about being more fully who you are.

Let yourself be seen - not for approval, but for authenticity. Let yourself be loved - not because you're perfect, but because you're present. The more you relax into your essence, the more you draw in people, opportunities, and relationships that honor that essence.

Emotional Intimacy and the Art of Vulnerable Expression

The feminine thrives in depth. In nuance. In the rich textures of emotional truth. Emotional intimacy is one of the deepest gifts we can offer and receive in relationship, yet it is also one of the most terrifying. It requires us to be seen - not just in our strength, but in our tenderness. Not just in our clarity, but in our confusion.

Vulnerability is often mistaken for weakness, but in truth, it is a profound strength. It takes courage to say, "I don't know." "That hurt me." "I need support." "I feel afraid." When you express your inner world without blaming, controlling, or expecting a specific response, you open the door to true intimacy.

The feminine communicates not just through words, but through energy, tone, gesture, and silence. She speaks in layers. In order to be heard, she must be willing to translate her feelings into language without betraying their depth. This is an art - and like all art, it requires practice.

One powerful tool is the use of "I" statements. Rather than saying, "You make me feel ignored," try, "When I don't feel acknowledged, I notice sadness and the desire to feel connected." This approach invites dialogue rather than defensiveness. It takes ownership of your feelings while opening space for the other to meet you.

Another key to emotional intimacy is presence. Put away distractions. Listen not just to words, but to what is underneath. Allow for silence. Ask deeper questions. Hold space not to fix, but to witness. The feminine is a deep ocean - and she longs to be met with depth, not solutions.

This is true in romantic relationships, but also in friendships, family dynamics, and community. Emotional intimacy is not exclusive to lovers - it is available wherever there is courage to be seen and willingness to see.

Let your emotions be pathways to connection, not obstacles. Let your vulnerability be a bridge, not a burden. When you speak from your heart, without agenda, you create the conditions for love to deepen.

Closing Invitation

The feminine in relationship is not about giving up power or gaining it. It is about embodying a way of relating that honors both self and other. That knows how to hold and be held. That knows when to open and when to pause. That trusts that connection does not require compromise of truth - but is strengthened by it.

Let your boundaries be sacred. Let your magnetism be your gift. Let your emotions be the map to deeper connection.

You are not too much for the right people. You are not too sensitive to be loved. You are not too complex to be understood.

You are exactly enough for relationships that honor the sacred.

Show up as you are.

Speak with your whole self.

Relate from your root, your heart, your essence.

This is the feminine path - not to lose yourself in another, but to find yourself more fully in the mirror of relationship.

Chapter 16: Creative Flow as Channel: Art, Dance, and Intuition as Forms of Divine Download

Creativity is not a luxury. It is not something reserved for artists or performers or those with specific talents. Creativity is life force moving through form, and it is one of the most powerful expressions of the feminine. It is the river beneath the surface of your thoughts, the whisper behind your breath, the sensation that nudges you to make something that has never existed before. In feminine wisdom traditions, creativity is not measured by output - it is honored as channeling. A woman in her creative flow is not just making something beautiful; she is opening herself to the sacred, receiving intuitive messages, and birthing energy into matter. To reclaim creative flow is to reclaim access to the divine within. Whether through writing, painting, dancing, singing, gardening, or daydreaming, this chapter invites you to trust your creative channel - not as a product to monetize or perfect, but as a mystical conversation between you and the mystery.

Creativity as Feminine Intelligence

The feminine creates from the body, from the senses, from the subconscious, and from the void. She does not follow straight lines or rigid instructions. She spirals, weaves, blends, feels, and trusts. Her process is rarely linear, and yet it is always rich with meaning. This is why feminine creativity often defies rules and explanations. It is intuitive, emotional, embodied. It moves in waves, not timelines.

Many people believe they are not creative because they don't paint or write or play music. But creativity is not defined by art forms. It lives in the way you dress, the way you speak, the way you solve problems, cook meals, make love, raise children, and design your life. Creativity is any moment when your soul meets the material world with presence and playfulness.

When we suppress our creativity, we suppress a vital part of our feminine essence. Often this suppression comes from early messages - "You're not good at this," "That's not practical," "Don't waste time on that," or "You're being too emotional." Over time, we begin to separate from our creative impulse. We learn to produce, but we forget how to create.

To return to feminine creative flow, we must first release the inner critic and embrace the sacred mess. Creativity doesn't require permission or perfection. It requires space. Spaciousness in the body, time, and mind. When we stop trying to control what comes through us and start listening to what wants to come, we begin to remember our true creative power.

This remembrance is deeply healing. When we create from a place of presence, we become whole. We bring together the parts of us that have been scattered - our inner child, our dreams, our desires, our emotions. We give them shape, color, sound. We let them speak.

Creative flow is not about making something "good." It's about allowing something true.

Embodied Creation: Movement and Dance

One of the most potent and accessible gateways to feminine creativity is the body. Movement bypasses the mind and opens the channel directly through sensation, rhythm, and energy. When we dance, stretch, sway, or move freely, we are not just exercising - we are listening. We are translating what lives inside into form.

Dance has always been part of feminine ritual. In temples of Isis, in the desert gatherings of Sufi women, in Indigenous ceremonies, and in sacred rites across the world, women moved together as prayer. Dance was a way to commune with spirit, to process emotion, to tell stories, and to release what the body could no longer hold.

You don't need choreography to access this. Embodied creation begins with listening. Close your eyes. Put on music that moves you. Let your body lead. Don't perform - feel. Let your hips sway, your arms rise, your feet stomp, your heart crack open. Let yourself move as you are, not as you think you should be.

Even five minutes of free movement can shift your energy profoundly. It clears stagnation, awakens the creative field, and re-centers your nervous system. This is why many women find inspiration after dancing - it's not because they've "earned" it, but because they've opened to it.

Movement also helps us release the shame we carry around our bodies and self-expression. The more we allow ourselves to move without judgment, the more we begin to trust our own rhythms. We stop seeking validation outside and begin to source joy and expression from within.

Let your dance be your medicine. Let your body be your brush. Let movement be the way you channel what words cannot yet say.

Intuition as the Creative Muse

Creativity is often described as inspiration, but for the feminine, it is more accurately described as intuition. Intuition is the deep knowing that arises without explanation. It is the quiet inner voice that suggests an image, a phrase, a color, a melody. It is the tug to try something, to follow an idea, to begin without knowing the end.

The feminine creative process is intimately connected to this intuitive flow. Rather than planning every detail, she listens. She follows clues. She honors the pauses. She understands that what is being created already exists in some form - her job is not to invent it, but to reveal it.

To work with creativity as a channel means creating time for silence. For receiving. It means trusting the nudges that don't make logical sense. It means writing down that dream image, sketching that shape that keeps appearing, singing that line that popped into your head while cooking. These are breadcrumbs from the intuitive realm.

You don't need to wait for the perfect idea or the right moment. The act of beginning is the signal that opens the channel wider. When you sit with your canvas, your notebook, your instrument, or your garden and say, "I'm listening," something always arrives. It may not be what you expected, but it will be what is needed.

One of the most powerful practices is to create without agenda. Set a timer for fifteen minutes and write, draw, or dance without editing or judging. Let your intuition guide you. Afterwards, reflect on what emerged. Often, our most profound insights come not from planning, but from surrender.

The feminine muse is not external. She lives in your belly, your breath, your blood, your dreams. She is not demanding. She is waiting. Waiting for your presence. Your trust. Your willingness to follow her into the unknown.

Closing Invitation

Your creativity is not a side project. It is not frivolous or optional. It is essential. It is the river that connects your spirit to the world. The channel through which the unseen becomes seen. The way your soul reminds you: I am alive.

Let yourself create badly. Let yourself make beauty without reason. Let yourself follow the thread even when you don't know where it leads.

You are not here to repeat what's already been done. You are here to express something only you can. That expression might take the form of a painting, a poem, a business, a garden, a home, a way of being. All of it is valid. All of it is sacred.

Trust your flow.

Follow your muse.

Open to receive what wants to move through you.

You are not just the artist - you are the canvas, the brush, the prayer, and the birth.

PART V: TRANSMITTING THE BLESSINGS

Chapter 17: Raising Feminine Children (Regardless of Gender): Nurturing Presence, Softness, and Inner Knowing

The world we create tomorrow begins with how we raise the children of today. And if we are to restore the balance of the sacred feminine in the world, it must begin not only within ourselves, but in how we guide the next generation. The feminine is not bound by gender; it is an energy, a quality of being that lives in all people. Every child, regardless of identity or expression, holds within them the potential for softness, empathy, creativity, intuition, and deep presence. These are not secondary traits. They are core aspects of human wholeness. Yet too often, children are taught to suppress their feelings, compete instead of connect, and push through rather than pause. This chapter offers a new perspective: to raise children in alignment with the sacred feminine is to raise them with reverence for their inner world. It is to teach them to feel, to listen, to imagine, to trust - and to know that their value is not measured in performance, but in presence.

Honoring Emotions as Sacred Language

Children are born emotionally fluent. They laugh loudly, cry freely, scream when frustrated, and love without reservation. But as they grow, many are taught - consciously or unconsciously - to silence this natural wisdom. "Stop crying." "Don't be so sensitive." "Calm down." These messages, though often well-meaning, teach children to disconnect from their emotional landscape rather than navigate it.

To raise children in the feminine way means honoring emotion as sacred, not shameful. It means seeing tears as intelligence, not weakness. It means teaching children not to suppress their feelings, but to understand them. When we make space for emotion, we teach resilience. When we name and validate feelings, we help children build emotional vocabulary, which in turn creates inner safety.

When a child is upset, rather than rushing to fix or distract, try simply being present. "I see that you're feeling really sad right now. That's okay. I'm here." This kind of witnessing doesn't deny the feeling - it allows it to move through. Children learn by example. When they see adults meeting emotion with compassion, they learn to do the same for themselves.

It's also important to create rituals for emotional expression. Journaling, drawing, dancing, singing - these are all forms of release and reflection. Encourage children to explore how they feel through art and storytelling. Let them know that their emotions are not problems to solve but messengers to listen to.

In doing so, we cultivate emotionally intelligent humans - people who can navigate complexity, connect with empathy, and honor their inner lives. These are the adults who will one day hold space for others, lead with compassion, and dare to be vulnerable in a world that often rewards the opposite.

Fostering Intuition, Imagination, and Inner Trust

Every child is born intuitive. They sense energy before they understand language. They know when something feels off, even if they can't explain why. They imagine freely, communicate with the unseen, and create elaborate worlds from the simplest materials. But over time, society teaches them to value logic over instinct, facts over feeling, and external validation over inner knowing.

Raising children in alignment with the feminine means protecting and nurturing their intuitive sense. This doesn't mean rejecting logic or structure, but it does mean making space for mystery, imagination, and the inner voice. Ask your children what their dreams were, what animals they feel connected to, what they sense in their bodies when making choices. These conversations invite self-trust.

Encourage unstructured time - moments where nothing is planned, and the child can simply explore, play, and discover. This is where intuition develops. When children are constantly directed, scheduled, and assessed, they lose the opportunity to hear their own internal signals. Boredom is not a problem - it's a gateway to creativity.

Storytelling is another powerful tool. Read myths, folktales, and stories from diverse cultures that emphasize inner strength, empathy, transformation, and mystery. These tales speak directly to the child's intuitive psyche and provide symbolic language for inner growth. Better still, invite your child to tell their own stories. This act reinforces the idea that their voice and vision matter.

Imagination is not just for play - it is a rehearsal space for life. When a child imagines being a healer, an artist, a dragon rider, or a tree whisperer, they are practicing courage, connection, and belief. Don't correct their imagination - honor it. Ask questions. Play along. Let them lead.

Children who trust their intuition grow into adults who can navigate uncertainty with confidence. They become decision-makers who align with their values, not just their fears. And in a world full of noise, those who can hear their inner voice are the ones who change the world.

Teaching Boundaries, Consent, and Embodied Self-Respect

A key part of raising children in the feminine is teaching them that their body is their own. That their no is sacred. That their yes must come from within. Boundaries, consent, and embodied awareness are foundational to feminine sovereignty - and they begin in childhood.

Teach children early that they have a right to say no. This includes affection. If a child does not want to hug or kiss someone - even a grandparent - they should not be forced to. Instead, teach alternatives: a wave, a high-five, or simply a smile. This reinforces the idea that affection is chosen, not owed.

Model consent in your own interactions. Ask before picking them up, interrupting their play, or helping them change clothes. These small gestures communicate that their body is respected. Over time, this builds an internal compass that will help them recognize healthy and unhealthy dynamics later in life.

Body awareness is also key. Invite your child to check in with their body throughout the day. Ask, "How does your belly feel right now?" or "What's your body saying it needs?" This helps develop the skill of tuning in and responding from the inside out.

Teach them to name and honor their needs. Whether it's a need for space, for comfort, for solitude, or for movement, these needs are not problems - they are wisdom. Help them identify when they feel safe, when they feel overwhelmed, and what helps them feel grounded. Give them tools - breathing, shaking, humming, drawing, journaling - that help them return to themselves.

And perhaps most importantly, teach them that they don't have to be perfect to be loved. That mistakes are not failures but invitations to learn. That their worth is not conditional on behavior or achievement. This deep knowing - of being inherently lovable - is the soil in which sovereignty grows.

Children who grow up with these teachings become adults who can self-regulate without suppressing, who can express without harming, and who can relate without losing themselves. They carry the codes of the feminine not as ideas, but as ways of being.

Closing Invitation

Raising feminine children is not about raising "soft" or "passive" children. It is about raising humans who are whole - who know how to feel, to imagine, to respect themselves and others, and to move through the world with both sensitivity and strength.

Whether you are a parent, teacher, aunt, uncle, or simply a conscious adult, you have the power to be a guardian of this sacred flame. The children are watching us - not just what we say, but how we live. When we treat our own emotions with care, trust our own intuition, and walk in self-respect, we show them what is possible.

The feminine does not need to be taught to children - it already lives in them. Our role is to protect it, to mirror it, to make room for it to grow.

Let your home be a temple of listening.

Let your presence be a blessing of safety.

Let your love be the soil where the sacred child remembers who they are.

And may the children we raise carry the feminine forward - not as a trend, but as a timeless truth that heals the world.

Chapter 18: The Feminine Leader: Leading Without Force: Influence Through Energy, Space, and Vision

Leadership has long been defined by traits rooted in masculine energy - assertiveness, control, strategy, dominance, and speed. While these qualities are not inherently negative, they tell only half the story. The feminine way of leading is less about command and more about coherence. It is not rooted in force, but in frequency. The feminine leader does not push her way forward; she magnetizes, guides, nurtures, and shapes the space around her through presence. She leads from intuition, not just intellect. From vision, not just planning. She listens deeply, moves cyclically, and invites others into transformation rather than directing them toward a goal. Feminine leadership is needed now more than ever - in business, in community, in family, and in self. This chapter redefines leadership not as a title or position, but as a way of being. And it invites all of us, regardless of gender or vocation, to lead from the inside out.

Energetic Leadership: Presence Before Performance

The most powerful tool a feminine leader possesses is her energy. Long before she speaks, decides, or acts, her energy communicates. It creates safety or tension, flow or friction. Feminine leadership begins with energetic self-awareness - attuning not just to what she's doing, but to how she's being.

In a culture that rewards urgency and productivity, the feminine leader returns to presence. She asks: What is the energy I'm bringing into this space? Am I grounded? Am I clear? Am I connected to my truth? She knows that leadership is not about managing others first - it is about managing her own state of being.

This kind of energy management is not a performance. It is not about masking emotion or pretending to be calm. It is about regulation, embodiment, and honesty. The feminine leader doesn't suppress what she feels - she integrates it. She breathes into it. She asks what it's teaching her. Then she moves from a place of wholeness, not fragmentation.

Because she is deeply attuned, she senses the unspoken. She notices when a room feels off, when a team is disconnected, when an idea lacks soul. She uses her intuition to guide her decisions, knowing that logic is necessary - but not sufficient. The feminine way of leading includes the unseen: dreams, body signals, synchronicities, ancestral wisdom.

Her presence is the field she holds. When she walks into a room, others feel the difference. Not because she demands attention, but because she radiates coherence. She has done the inner work. She trusts her inner compass. And in doing so, she becomes a lighthouse for others - not by controlling their ships, but by shining steadily in her own truth.

Holding Space Instead of Taking Control

Traditional models of leadership often involve taking charge - making decisions, giving orders, and being at the center. But feminine leadership turns this model inside out. Instead of occupying the center, she creates a container. She holds space, allowing others to rise within it.

Holding space is not passive. It requires strength, boundaries, and clarity. But it is a different kind of strength - a receptive strength, a stabilizing force. It means being able to sit in discomfort without rushing to fix. It means witnessing others in their growth without needing to impose your agenda. It means cultivating a field where transformation can unfold organically.

Whether leading a business, a classroom, a household, or a spiritual circle, the feminine leader creates rituals of safety. She listens more than she speaks. She invites collaboration instead of competition. She welcomes diverse voices and knows that collective intelligence is more powerful than individual control.

This doesn't mean she lacks direction. She has vision - but she's not attached to a rigid pathway. She allows the journey to unfold, adapting as needed, trusting the timing, and knowing that detours often hold the deeper wisdom.

She creates environments where others feel seen, valued, and empowered. In her presence, people remember their own worth. They feel free to bring their whole selves - messy, radiant, real. Because she is not threatened by other people's power, she cultivates it.

And when conflict arises - as it always does - she meets it with compassion and clarity. She does not avoid difficult conversations, but she doesn't weaponize them either. She creates space for truth, for repair, for reconciliation. Her leadership does not seek to dominate. It seeks to liberate.

Leading with Vision and Embodiment

Feminine leadership is visionary. But unlike ego-driven visions, which seek success for recognition, the feminine vision arises from service. From love. From the desire to birth something meaningful into the world. Her vision is often felt before it is fully understood. It begins in the body, in the womb, in the dream. It stirs her heart and will not let her rest until it is spoken.

To lead with vision means to trust what you cannot fully explain. To walk toward something that lives more in feeling than in form. The feminine leader knows that visions gestate like life itself - they take time, they require nourishment, and they cannot be rushed. She holds the vision not as a demand, but as a prayer.

She also embodies the change she seeks. Rather than preaching values, she lives them. If she teaches rest, she rests. If she teaches self-love, she loves herself in her fullness. If she calls for authenticity, she dares to be seen in her truth. Her leadership is not a message - it is a transmission.

This embodiment gives her credibility. Not because she's perfect, but because she is aligned. Her life becomes her teaching. Her presence becomes her leadership. People are drawn to her not just for what she does, but for how she makes them feel - safe, inspired, empowered, and connected.

Feminine vision also includes the relational. It is not individualistic. She asks: How will this decision affect the collective? How can we rise together? How can we create systems that honor the earth, the body, and the soul?

She is not afraid to dream bigger. But her dreams are not based on conquest. They are based on coherence. A world where people are free to be who they are. Where feminine and masculine energies are in balance. Where leadership is measured not by control, but by consciousness.

Closing Invitation

You do not need a title to be a leader. You do not need a degree, a following, or permission. You lead every time you choose presence over pressure. Every time you hold space instead of rushing to fix. Every time you embody the values you want to see in the world.

Feminine leadership is not about having power over others. It's about standing in your own power so that others remember theirs. It's about creating spaces where truth can flourish, where collaboration replaces competition, and where vision arises from soul.

Let your energy speak before your words.

Let your presence shape the room.

Let your integrity be your message.

You are not here to lead like anyone else. You are here to lead like only you can.

Softly. Fiercely. Fully.

Lead with your body. Lead with your heart. Lead with your whole self.

This is how the feminine returns - not just in spirit, but in action.

Chapter 19: Creating Blessing Altars: Personal Sacred Spaces That Shift Your Frequency

There is something timeless and deeply human about building an altar. Across cultures, geographies, and belief systems, altars have always existed as places of connection, intention, and transformation. They are not merely decorative corners filled with trinkets; they are energetic anchors - spaces where the unseen becomes seen, where the ordinary becomes sacred, and where we remember that we are not separate from the divine. In the feminine tradition, creating a blessing altar is an act of devotion, not to a distant god, but to life itself. It is a practice that invites presence, beauty, and ritual into the home and heart. An altar is where you go to return to yourself. In this chapter, you will be guided to understand the purpose and power of altars, how to create one that reflects your essence, and how to use it as a living, breathing tool for aligning your energy, intentions, and feminine frequency.

The Meaning and Energy of an Altar

An altar is a visible reminder of the invisible. It is where the soul meets the senses. Through color, texture, scent, sound, and symbolic form, an altar creates a field of energy that draws us into deeper presence. Whether large or small, permanent or mobile, simple or ornate, it becomes a focal point for connection - with ourselves, with the divine, with the earth, with our ancestors, or with a specific intention.

The feminine path does not require a temple or priesthood to feel sacred. She knows that the sacred is wherever you decide to honor it. An altar can be a shelf, a tray, a corner of a desk, a garden nook, or even a collection of meaningful objects placed together in your bag or car. What matters is not how it looks, but how it feels.

The energy of an altar is shaped by your presence. When you tend to it, speak to it, or simply sit before it in silence, you are not worshipping an object - you are charging a space with attention and intention. Over time, this becomes a portal. The more you use it, the more it "remembers" and holds your frequency.

There is no single right way to create an altar, because it is an extension of your own spiritual language. What calls to you? What materials, textures, or colors feel alive to your soul? What objects remind you of who you truly are? The process of gathering these elements is in itself a ritual. You are not just decorating a space - you are reclaiming a sacred conversation.

When you walk past your altar, it should whisper to you. Remind you. Ground you. Inspire you. Like a beloved elder or a sacred mirror, it offers presence without judgment, holding space for your becoming.

How to Create a Feminine Blessing Altar

Creating a blessing altar begins with listening. Before you place a single object, take time to feel into your intention. What do you want this altar to support or reflect? Is it for daily grounding? A specific life transition? A connection with the moon, with your ancestors, with your creativity? Let your why guide your what.

Choose a location that feels accessible and peaceful. This could be a quiet corner of your bedroom, a windowsill with natural light, a meditation space, or even a mobile altar you carry in a pouch. Cleanse the area physically and energetically. You might smudge with herbs, spray essential oils, or simply clap your hands and speak aloud your intention to create sacred space.

Begin to gather elements that carry meaning. These may include:

- Candles to represent light, fire, and transformation

- Crystals for grounding, clarity, or amplification
- Feathers, shells, stones, or sand to represent the elements
- A bowl of water to hold emotion and reflection
- Photos or items connected to your lineage or guides
- Flowers or leaves to connect with natural cycles
- Written prayers, affirmations, or intentions
- Sacred symbols or talismans
- A cloth or textile that brings beauty and color

Arrange your altar intuitively. There is no need to overthink the layout. Let your hands guide you. Notice where your eyes rest, where your breath softens. You are creating not just a visual space, but an energetic field. If something feels off, adjust until you feel harmony.

Once complete, take a moment to activate the altar. Light the candle. Speak your intention. Breathe with the space. You might place your hands over your heart and then onto the altar itself, offering your energy and receiving its presence in return.

Remember that your altar is not static - it is a living space. Let it change with the seasons, your moods, your needs. Refresh it with fresh flowers, new objects, or different intentions. Just as the feminine is cyclical, so too can your altar evolve. Let it reflect your inner landscape.

Return to it often. Even if just for a minute each day. Sit in silence. Ask a question. Cry. Journal. Sing. Offer gratitude. Your altar will not judge - it will receive. Over time, it becomes more than a space. It becomes a sacred companion.

Using Your Altar to Shift Frequency and Manifest Intention

An altar is not just a pretty setup - it is a spiritual technology. When used with intention, it becomes a tool for frequency alignment and manifestation. Your frequency is the sum of your thoughts, emotions, embodiment, and energetic field. When you enter into relationship with your altar, you consciously shift that field.

Start by approaching the altar when you are emotionally scattered, overwhelmed, or disconnected. Simply placing your hands on your altar or taking a few breaths before it can help regulate your nervous system and realign your inner compass. The space itself carries the energetic imprint of your intention - stepping into it reminds your body of what is true.

You can also use the altar as a site of ritual manifestation. For example, if you are calling in a creative project, you might place a symbol of that project on the altar - a pen, a paintbrush, a piece of paper with a title written on it. Every time you light a candle before it, you are anchoring that vision into the physical world.

Likewise, if you are in a period of grief or transition, your altar can become a space to honor release. You might write a letter to what you're letting go of and place it beneath a stone. Or you might light a candle each day in remembrance. These small, symbolic acts carry profound energetic weight. They speak to the subconscious and soul alike.

The key is consistency. Return to the altar even when you don't "feel" like it. The feminine is not about performance, but about relationship. Your altar is not a chore. It is a place to come home.

And over time, you will notice something subtle but powerful: your outer world begins to respond to your inner frequency. As you shift within, life begins to reorganize around your new vibration. This is not magic in the fantastical sense - it is resonance. Your altar is your tuning fork. It helps you remember your note and sing it into being.

Closing Invitation

In a world that rushes, distracts, and fragments, creating a blessing altar is an act of sacred rebellion. It says: I choose to live in connection. I choose beauty, intention, and reverence. I choose to walk with the sacred, not only in temples, but in my daily life.

You don't need to wait for someone to initiate you. You don't need permission. You are the priestess. You are the guide. You are the one who remembers how to tend to the flame.

Let your altar be your sanctuary. Your mirror. Your magic.

Let it hold your grief, your joy, your desire, your dreams.

Let it change as you change.

Let it remind you that the sacred is never far - it is wherever you choose to see it.

This is how we weave the feminine back into the fabric of our lives - not through grand gestures, but through daily devotion.

You are the blessing.

Your life is the altar.

Let it be lit.

Chapter 20: Your Feminine Legacy: A Final Guided Practice to Anchor Your Own Ancient Blessing into the World

Legacy is often spoken of in terms of what we leave behind - achievements, possessions, influence. But in the feminine way, legacy is not measured in numbers or accolades. It is energetic. It is what we imprint upon the fabric of life through the way we love, listen, create, heal, and show up. Your feminine legacy is not just what you do - it is who you become. It is not something far in the future, tied to age or death. It begins now, in the way you live, in the energy you carry, in the blessings you embody and transmit daily. This chapter is not about planning your impact; it is about anchoring your presence. It is a call to remember that you are a bridge - between past and future, spirit and matter, seen and unseen. You carry ancient codes in your body. You are the living altar of your lineage. And the more you root into that truth, the more your very life becomes a blessing to the world.

Listening to the Thread of Your Lineage

To understand your feminine legacy, you must begin by acknowledging the thread you come from. No matter your family story - whether it is one of deep connection or of rupture - there is a lineage behind you. Women and feminine beings who came before you. Some were mothers. Some were creators, healers, outcasts, midwives, priestesses, warriors, poets. Some were silenced. Some were powerful. Some forgot. Some remembered.

Your body carries their stories. Your instincts, your fears, your talents, your longings - they are not all yours alone. They are echoes of those who walked before. Your task is not to carry their burdens, but to listen to their wisdom. To honor what wants to move through you. To reclaim the threads that were cut. To let go of the ones that were never yours to hold.

You can begin this practice simply. Sit in a quiet space, perhaps before your altar or in nature. Close your eyes. Take a few deep breaths. Call to your maternal and paternal lineages. Say aloud or silently: "I honor those who came before me. I am listening." Wait. Feel. Let images, emotions, or sensations arise.

You may see faces. You may feel waves of energy. You may remember a grandmother's voice, a scent from childhood, a story long buried. Or you may feel nothing - and that's okay. The work is subtle, but real. You are opening the ancestral gate.

When you're ready, ask: "What gift am I carrying forward?" Listen again. It might be a word, a color, an emotion, an image. Let it speak to you. This gift is part of your feminine legacy. It is what your lineage wants to give through you - not just to your descendants, but to the wider world.

You are not here to repeat the past. You are here to redeem it, evolve it, and reweave it with conscious love. By embodying your truth, you bless those behind you and light the way for those to come.

Living as the Blessing You Are

The core of your feminine legacy is not about doing more. It's about being more deeply who you already are. When you walk in integrity, when you live in rhythm, when you honor your needs, your emotions, your body, your soul - you radiate a frequency that changes the field around you.

The modern world often makes us feel like we have to achieve worthiness, climb toward meaning, or chase purpose. But the feminine way says: You are already whole. You are already the channel. You are already the blessing. The more you trust that, the more your life becomes a transmission.

This doesn't mean you don't have dreams or desires - it means that your essence is not dependent on them. You don't need a platform, a title, a perfect plan. You need only to be aligned, embodied, and present. The impact you make is not in what you claim, but in what you carry.

Every time you soften when you want to harden, you create legacy.
Every time you tell the truth instead of perform, you create legacy.
Every time you honor your cycle, your rest, your knowing, you create legacy.
Every time you forgive yourself, you free your bloodline.
Every time you light a candle in the dark, you remind the world that light exists.

The feminine does not create legacy by force. She does it by resonance. By walking in beauty. By loving deeply. By living in ceremony. And most of all, by not abandoning herself.

If you've been waiting for a sign, for the right moment, for the invitation - this is it. Your very breath is enough. Your presence is the altar. Your authenticity is the offering.

Let yourself be the blessing you were born to carry. Let it live in your words, your movements, your choices, your silence. Let your life be your sacred legacy.

Anchoring Your Blessing: A Guided Practice

Now that you've explored the concept of your feminine legacy, it's time to ground it with a practice. This ritual is meant to help you claim and activate the unique blessing you are here to embody and transmit. You may do this alone, or in circle with others.

Begin by preparing a sacred space. You may want your altar nearby, a candle, journal, and any objects that feel supportive - a scarf, a flower, a stone. Dress in something that makes you feel like your truest self. Let the space feel intimate and alive.

Sit comfortably and close your eyes. Take several slow, deep breaths. Drop into your body. Feel the ground beneath you. Feel your spine as a bridge between earth and sky.

Silently or aloud, say

"I call forth the blessing that lives in me.

I call forth the thread of wisdom that I am here to carry.

I call forth the part of me that remembers who I am."

Pause. Feel. Listen.

Now bring to mind the word, phrase, or feeling that has followed you throughout this book - or throughout your life. What is the energy you most deeply carry? Is it compassion? Clarity? Sensuality? Stillness? Truth? Creativity? Healing?

Name it. Whisper it. Own it.

Say:

"This is my feminine blessing.

This is the frequency I am here to live.

I choose to anchor it, not only in words, but in action."

Now place your hands over your heart. Imagine that this blessing is a light, a frequency, a seed inside you. Feel it grow with each breath. You may want to journal about how this blessing wants to move through you - in your relationships, your work, your rituals, your choices.

You are now the guardian of this blessing. You are not here to be perfect - you are here to be present. To live in alignment with what you carry. And in doing so, to ripple out healing, remembrance, and possibility into the world.

Close the ritual by placing your hands on the earth or on your altar. Offer gratitude. Say aloud:

"May my life be a prayer.

May my presence be a legacy.

May my blessing live through all I touch."

Take a final breath, and when ready, return to the day - anchored, aligned, and aware that your presence is sacred.

Closing Words

This is not the end. It is the beginning of a new embodiment.

You have walked through myths, memories, practices, cycles, rituals, wounds, wisdoms, and rebirths. You have remembered what was never lost - only sleeping.

Now you walk with the feminine not as an idea, but as a frequency. As a path. As a blessing.

Carry it with humility. With courage. With joy.

Let your life speak what cannot be spoken.

Let your body become the hymn.

Let your breath be the drumbeat of remembrance.

This is your feminine legacy - not a monument, but a movement.

Not a crown, but a current.

Not someday, but now.

May it flow through you.

May it outlive you.

May it bless the world.

www.ingramcontent.com/pod-product-compliance
Lightning Source LLC
Chambersburg PA
CBHW072159160426
43197CB00012B/2456